n Beha Architects · Anshen+Allen · Biesek Design · Cannon Design · CO Architects · Derck & Edson Associates · DiMella Shaffer · Earl Swensson Associates,
Sa) · Elkus Manfredi Architects · ELS Architecture and Urban Design · Gould Evans · GUND Rupert Ainge Inc. · Hastings & Chive
MC Architects · HOLT Architects, P.C. · Kallmann McKinnell & Wood Architects, Inc. · Perkins si Associa
BLD Studio · Schuler Shook · Selbert Perkins Design · Steven Holl Architects · Tai Soo Kim l Architect
nn Beha Architects · Anshen+Allen · Biesek Design · Cannon Design · CO Architects · D on Associat
(ESa) · Elkus Manfredi Architects · ELS Architecture and Urban Design · Gould Evans Hasting
ivetta · HMC Architects · HOLT Architects, P.C. · Kallmann McKinnell & Wood Architects, Inc Roll • Barr
sociates · SBLD Studio · Schuler Shook · Selbert Perkins Design · Steven Holl Architects · Tai Soo Kim Partners · VOA Associates Incorporated · Yost Grube H
chitecture · Ann Beha Architects · Anshen+Allen · Biesek Design · Cannon Design · CO Architects · Derck & Edson Associates · DiMella Shaffer · Earl Swens
sociates, Inc. (ESa) · Elkus Manfredi Architects · ELS Architecture and Urban Design · Gould Evans · GUND Partnership · Hammond Beeby Rupert Ainge Inc
stings & Chivetta · HMC Architects · HOLT Architects, P.C. · Kallmann McKinnell & Wood Architects, Inc. · Perkins Eastman · Perkins+Will · Poulin + Morris Inc
l • Barresi Associates · SBLD Studio · Schuler Shook · Selbert Perkins Design · Steven Holl Architects · Tai Soo Kim Partners · VOA Associates Incorporate
st Grube Hall Architecture · Ann Beha Architects · Anshen+Allen · Biesek Design · Cannon Design · CO Architects · Derck & Edson Associates · DiMella Shaffe
rl Swensson Associates, Inc. (ESa) · Elkus Manfredi Architects · ELS Architecture and Urban Design · Gould Evans · GUND Partnership · Hammond Beeby Rup
ge Inc. · Hastings & Chivetta · HMC Architects · HOLT Architects, P.C. · Kallmann McKinnell & Wood Architects, Inc. · Perkins Eastman · Perkins+Will · Pouli
rris Inc. · Roll • Barresi Associates · SBLD Studio · Schuler Shook · Selbert Perkins Design · Steven Holl Architects · Tai Soo Kim Partners · VOA Associa
orporated · Yost Grube Hall Architecture · Ann Beha Architects · Anshen+Allen · Biesek Design · Cannon Design · CO Architects · Derck & Edson Associate
Mella Shaffer · Earl Swensson Associates, Inc. (ESa) · Elkus Manfredi Architects · ELS Architecture and Urban Design · Gould Evans · GUND Partnership · Hammc
eby Rupert Ainge Inc. · Hastings & Chivetta · HMC Architects · HOLT Architects, P.C. · Kallmann McKinnell & Wood Architects, Inc. · Perkins Eastman · Perkins+V
Poulin + Morris Inc. · Roll • Barresi Associates · SBLD Studio · Schuler Shook · Selbert Perkins Design · Steven Holl Architects · Tai Soo Kim Partners · V
sociates Incorporated · Yost Grube Hall Architecture · Ann Beha Architects · Anshen+Allen · Biesek Design · Cannon Design · CO Architects · Derck & Eds
sociates · DiMella Shaffer · Earl Swensson Associates, Inc. (ESa) · Elkus Manfredi Architects · ELS Architecture and Urban Design · Gould Evans · GUND Partners
ammond Beeby Rupert Ainge Inc. · Hastings & Chivetta · HMC Architects · HOLT Architects, P.C. · Kallmann McKinnell & Wood Architects, Inc. · Perkins Eastn
erkins+Will · Poulin + Morris Inc. · Roll • Barresi Associates · SBLD Studio · Schuler Shook · Selbert Perkins Design · Steven Holl Architects · Tai Soo Kim Partn
OA Associates Incorporated · Yost Grube Hall Architecture · Ann Beha Architects · Anshen+Allen · Biesek Design · Cannon Design · CO Architects · Derc
son Associates · DiMella Shaffer · Earl Swensson Associates, Inc. (ESa) · Elkus Manfredi Architects · ELS Architecture and Urban Design · Gould Evans · GU
rtnership · Hammond Beeby Rupert Ainge Inc. · Hastings & Chivetta · HMC Architects · HOLT Architects, P.C. · Kallmann McKinnell & Wood Architects, Inc. · Perk
stman · Perkins+Will · Poulin + Morris Inc. · Roll • Barresi Associates · SBLD Studio · Schuler Shook · Selbert Perkins Design · Steven Holl Architects · Tai S
n Partners · VOA Associates Incorporated · Yost Grube Hall Architecture · Ann Beha Architects · Anshen+Allen · Biesek Design · Cannon Design · CO Archite
erck & Edson Associates · DiMella Shaffer · Earl Swensson Associates, Inc. (ESa) · Elkus Manfredi Architects · ELS Architecture and Urban Design · Gould Evar
ND Partnership · Hammond Beeby Rupert Ainge Inc. · Hastings & Chivetta · HMC Architects · HOLT Architects, P.C. · Kallmann McKinnell & Wood Architects,
erkins Eastman · Perkins+Will · Poulin + Morris Inc. · Roll • Barresi Associates · SBLD Studio · Schuler Shook · Selbert Perkins Design · Steven Holl Architec
Soo Kim Partners · VOA Associates Incorporated · Yost Grube Hall Architecture · Ann Beha Architects · Anshen+Allen · Biesek Design · Cannon Design ·
chitects · Derck & Edson Associates · DiMella Shaffer · Earl Swensson Associates, Inc. (ESa) · Elkus Manfredi Architects · ELS Architecture and Urban Desig
uld Evans · GUND Partnership · Hammond Beeby Rupert Ainge Inc. · Hastings & Chivetta · HMC Architects · HOLT Architects, P.C. · Kallmann McKinnell & Wo
chitects, Inc. · Perkins Eastman · Perkins+Will · Poulin + Morris Inc. · Roll • Barresi Associates · SBLD Studio · Schuler Shook · Selbert Perkins Design · Ste
ll Architects · Tai Soo Kim Partners · VOA Associates Incorporated · Yost Grube Hall Architecture · Ann Beha Architects · Anshen+Allen · Biesek Design · Cann
sign · CO Architects · Derck & Edson Associates · DiMella Shaffer · Earl Swensson Associates, Inc. (ESa) · Elkus Manfredi Architects · ELS Architecture and Ur
sign · Gould Evans · GUND Partnership · Hammond Beeby Rupert Ainge Inc. · Hastings & Chivetta · HMC Architects · HOLT Architects, P.C. · Kallmann McKin
Wood Architects, Inc. · Perkins Eastman · Perkins+Will · Poulin + Morris Inc. · Roll • Barresi Associates · SBLD Studio · Schuler Shook · Selbert Perkins Desig
even Holl Architects · Tai Soo Kim Partners · VOA Associates Incorporated · Yost Grube Hall Architecture · Ann Beha Architects · Anshen+Allen · Biesek Desig
nnon Design · CO Architects · Derck & Edson Associates · DiMella Shaffer · Earl Swensson Associates, Inc. (ESa) · Elkus Manfredi Architects · ELS Architect
d Urban Design · Gould Evans · GUND Partnership · Hammond Beeby Rupert Ainge Inc. · Hastings & Chivetta · HMC Architects · HOLT Architects, P.C. · Kallma
Kinnell & Wood Architects, Inc. · Perkins Eastman · Perkins+Will · Poulin + Morris Inc. · Roll • Barresi Associates · SBLD Studio · Schuler Shook · Selbert Perk
sign · Steven Holl Architects · Tai Soo Kim Partners · VOA Associates Incorporated · Yost Grube Hall Architecture · Ann Beha Architects · Anshen+Allen · Bie
sign · Cannon Design · CO Architects · Derck & Edson Associates · DiMella Shaffer · Earl Swensson Associates, Inc. (ESa) · Elkus Manfredi Architects · E
chitecture and Urban Design · Gould Evans · GUND Partnership · Hammond Beeby Rupert Ainge Inc. · Hastings & Chivetta · HMC Architects · HOLT Archite
. · Kallmann McKinnell & Wood Architects, Inc. · Perkins Eastman · Perkins+Will · Poulin + Morris Inc. · Roll • Barresi Associates · SBLD Studio · Schuler Sh
Selbert Perkins Design · Steven Holl Architects · Tai Soo Kim Partners · VOA Associates Incorporated · Yost Grube Hall Architecture · Ann Beha Architect
shen+Allen · Biesek Design · Cannon Design · CO Architects · Derck & Edson Associates · DiMella Shaffer · Earl Swensson Associates, Inc. (ESa) · Elkus Manfr
chitects · ELS Architecture and Urban Design · Gould Evans · GUND Partnership · Hammond Beeby Rupert Ainge Inc. · Hastings & Chivetta · HMC Architec
LT Architects, P.C. · Kallmann McKinnell & Wood Architects, Inc. · Perkins Eastman · Perkins+Will · Poulin + Morris Inc. · Roll • Barresi Associates · SBLD Stu
Schuler Shook · Selbert Perkins Design · Steven Holl Architects · Tai Soo Kim Partners · VOA Associates Incorporated · Yost Grube Hall Architecture · Ann B
chitects · Anshen+Allen · Biesek Design · Cannon Design · CO Architects · Derck & Edson Associates · DiMella Shaffer · Earl Swensson Associates, Inc. (ES
kus Manfredi Architects · ELS Architecture and Urban Design · Gould Evans · GUND Partnership · Hammond Beeby Rupert Ainge Inc. · Hastings & Chivetta · H
chitects · HOLT Architects, P.C. · Kallmann McKinnell & Wood Architects, Inc. · Perkins Eastman · Perkins+Will · Poulin + Morris Inc. · Roll • Barresi Associate
LD Studio · Schuler Shook · Selbert Perkins Design · Steven Holl Architects · Tai Soo Kim Partners · VOA Associates Incorporated · Yost Grube Hall Architect
nn Beha Architects · Anshen+Allen · Biesek Design · Cannon Design · CO Architects · Derck & Edson Associates · DiMella Shaffer · Earl Swensson Associa
. (ESa) · Elkus Manfredi Architects · ELS Architecture and Urban Design · Gould Evans · GUND Partnership · Hammond Beeby Rupert Ainge Inc. · Hasting
ivetta · HMC Architects · HOLT Architects, P.C. · Kallmann McKinnell & Wood Architects, Inc. · Perkins Eastman · Perkins+Will · Poulin + Morris Inc. · Roll • Bar
sociates · SBLD Studio · Schuler Shook · Selbert Perkins Design · Steven Holl Architects · Tai Soo Kim Partners · VOA Associates Incorporated · Yost Grube
chitecture · Ann Beha Architects · Anshen+Allen · Biesek Design · Cannon Design · CO Architects · Derck & Edson Associates · DiMella Shaffer · Earl Swens
sociates, Inc. (ESa) · Elkus Manfredi Architects · ELS Architecture and Urban Design · Gould Evans · GUND Partnership · Hammond Beeby Rupert Ainge In
stings & Chivetta · HMC Architects · HOLT Architects, P.C. · Kallmann McKinnell & Wood Architects, Inc. · Perkins Eastman · Perkins+Will · Poulin + Morris In
l • Barresi Associates · SBLD Studio · Schuler Shook · Selbert Perkins Design · Steven Holl Architects · Tai Soo Kim Partners · VOA Associates Incorporate
st Grube Hall Architecture · Ann Beha Architects · Anshen+Allen · Biesek Design · Cannon Design · CO Architects · Derck & Edson Associates · DiMella Shaff
rl Swensson Associates, Inc. (ESa) · Elkus Manfredi Architects · ELS Architecture and Urban Design · Gould Evans · GUND Partnership · Hammond Beeby Rup
nge Inc. · Hastings & Chivetta · HMC Architects · HOLT Architects, P.C. · Kallmann McKinnell & Wood Architects, Inc. · Perkins Eastman · Perkins+Will · Poul
rris Inc · Roll • Barresi Associates · SBLD Studio · Schuler Shook · Selbert Perkins Design · Steven Holl Architects · Tai Soo Kim Partners · VOA Associa

Ann Beha Architects · Anshen+Allen · Biesek Design · Cannon Design · CO Architects · Derck & Edson Associates · DiMella Shaffer · Earl Swensson Associates, Inc. (ESa) · Elkus Manfredi Architects · ELS Architecture and Urban Design · Gould Evans · GUND Partnership · Hammond Beeby Rupert Ainge Inc. · Hastings & Chivetta · HMC Architects · HOLT Architects, P.C. · Kallmann McKinnell & Wood Architects, Inc. · Perkins Eastman · Perkins+Will · Poulin + Morris Inc. · Roll • Barresi Associates · SBLD Studio · Schuler Shook · Selbert Perkins Design · Steven Holl Architects · Tai Soo Kim Partners · VOA Associates Incorporated · Yost Grube Hall Architecture

Educational
Environments 4

Educational
Environments 4

Roger Yee

Visual Reference Publications Inc., New York

Opposite: Wesleyan University, Usdan University Center, Middletown, Connecticut. **Design firm:** Kallmann McKinnell & Wood Architects. **Photography:** Robert Benson.

Educational Environments 4

Visual Reference Publications, Inc.
302 Fifth Avenue • New York, NY 10001
Tel: 212.279.7000 • Fax: 212.279.7014 • Fax: 212.279.7014

www.visualreference.com

GROUP PUBLISHER	Larry Fuersich larry@visualreference.com
PUBLISHER	Bill Ash bill@visualreference.com
EDITORIAL DIRECTOR	Roger Yee yeerh@aol.com
CREATIVE ART DIRECTOR	Veronika Levin veronika@visualreference.com
ASSISTANT ART DIRECTORS	Martina Parisi martina@visualreference.com
PRODUCTION MANAGER	John Hogan johnhvrp@yahoo.com
CIRCULATION MANAGER	Amy-Mei Li amy@visualreference.com
MARKETING COORDINATOR	Nika Chopra nika@visualreference.com
CONTROLLER	Angie Goulimis angie@visualreference.com

ISBN: 978-1-58471-167-4

Distributors to the trade in the United States and Canada
Innovative Logistics
575 Prospect Street
Lakewood, NJ 08701
732.363.5679

Distributors outside the United States and Canada
HarperCollins International
10 East 53rd Street
New York, NY 10022-5299

Exclusive distributor in China
Beijing Designerbooks Co., Ltd.
B-0619, No.2 Building, Dacheng International Center
78 East 4th Ring Middle Road
Chaoyang District, Beijing 100022, P.R. China
Tel: 0086(010)5962-6195 Fax: 0086(010)5962-6193
E-mail: info@designerbooks.net www.designerbooks.net

Printed and bound in China

Book Design: Veronika Levin

The paper on which this book is printed contains
recycled content to support a sustainable world.

People say you should never sit on a good idea.
We tend to disagree.

EDUCATIONAL FURNITURE SOLUTIONS

CLASSROOM • COMPUTER ROOM • LIBRARY / MEDIA CENTER • AUDITORIUM / LECTURE HALL

Contents

Introduction

The Right Stuff

If the nation can solve such chronic problems as nearly a third of its youth failing to finish high school, innovative school design is setting the stage for a renaissance in American education

Fate, fortune and God's will notwithstanding, education was a key reason why the United States became the dominant 20th century economy. Believing education to be essential to self-improvement, America gave more people more education than other industrialized nations. The average adult's educational attainment ascended in step with the nation's productivity, wealth and power, from eight years of schooling in 1890 to 8.8 years in 1900, 9.6 years in 1910, and 14 years in 1960.

No wonder Americans were shocked in 1983 when the Reagan administration issued "A Nation at Risk." The report indicted the quality of American primary and secondary schools, providing an ominous drumbeat to an era when the United States lost its educational lead over economic rivals. Now, a quarter-century later, American fourth and eighth graders persistently score in the middle of the ranks of industrialized nations in mathematics, science and literacy, and 30 percent of young Americans fail to complete high school. In a global economy where Europe and Asia routinely challenge the United States for economic supremacy, these shortcomings are troubling.

Fortunately, there's no shortage of ideas for improving U.S. education. Giving teachers better preparation, ongoing training and support, and higher compensation, encouraging parents to be involved in their children's schooling, letting the public share facilities and costs, and motivating students through group-oriented inquiry and research and other learning methods are all good strategies. At the same time, we are building some of the most innovative educational facilities ever to support the new educational directives, and they're already making a difference.

Consider a sampling of the new educational environments from some of the leading architects, planners and designers in the field, whose work is shown on the following pages of EDUCATIONAL ENVIRONMENTS NO. 4.

Many of today's classrooms are flexible in dimensions, layout and equipment, allowing teachers and students to shape them in ways that foster critical thinking and open inquiry. Libraries no longer just store print and enforce silence, having welcomed new media, group study facilities and even cafés among the stacks and reading rooms. Laboratories place teachers, students and their work in high-technology settings surrounded by opportunities for scholarly exchange and social interaction, providing both the means for intensive, private effort—and an escape from it.

Change can also be experienced outside of school hours. Student unions and recreational centers acknowledge the importance of student life beyond classes by introducing opportunities for social and physical activities that attract students, faculty and alumni. Dormitories offer students unprecedented privacy and convenience along with informal sociability and community to ease the transition from home to campus. Performing arts centers open new realms of drama, dance and music to students while inviting community residents to share them.

Of course, good design won't guarantee better education in America. For that we need good teachers, motivated students and suppo rtive communities as well as solid schoolhouses. But what could be more American than wanting each new schoolhouse to be more functional, cost-effective, up-to-date and appealing than before? That's why, for example, many new projects in this book reflect green design strategies, making more efficient use of energy, water and sustainable materials, eliminating VOCs from interior finishes, and incorporating local climate conditions, building materials, and construction techniques whenever possible. Good design and good education make good company.

Roger Yee

Editor

Intelligent SOLUTIONS

Since 1886

The Leader in Opening Glass Walls

Sir Francis Drake High School   Student Center
San Anselmo, CA   Deems Lewis McKinley Architecture

Ann Beha Architects

33 Kingston Street • Boston, MA 02111 • 617.338.3000 • (F) 617.482.9097

www.annbeha.com

Ann Beha Architects

Bard College at Simon's Rock
Daniel Arts Center
Great Barrington, Massachusetts

Not your everyday liberal arts college, Bard College at Simon's Rock, in Great Barrington, Massachusetts, founded in 1966, educates 400 students from 10th or 11th grade at its distinctive, 275-acre campus. A recent addition, the award-winning, 53,000-square-foot Daniel Arts Center, designed by Ann Beha Architects, is similarly unique. Its three buildings are modern, angular forms combining wood siding and crisp metal detailing, with anodized aluminum windows and clear plastic cellular panels. Campus pathways are integrated into the building's corridors, creating an arts walk with informal pin-up galleries and views into studios, providing an opportunity for the whole campus community to become engaged with the production of the arts. The performing arts spaces are sandwiched between the Visual Arts Wing and the 3D Studio Shop. The Performing Arts Center contains a 350-seat Main Stage Theatre, 100-seat Studio Theatre, dance studio, lobby and support spaces. The Visual Arts Wing's "clean" arts include an electronic arts studio, "midi" sound studio, computer laboratories, photography, painting, drawing and printmaking spaces, classrooms and offices. The 3D Studio Shop offers metal and woodworking, set and assembly shops, ceramics, plaster and computer controlled modeling studios, offices, support spaces and is sited around an outdoor Arts Court. Yet, despite its newness, the Center nestles easily into its wooded sloping site as if it were always there.

Ann Beha Architects

University of Pennsylvania
David B. Weigle Information Commons in the
Van Pelt-Dietrich Library Center
Philadelphia, Pennsylvania

Left: Reception

Below right: Open work areas and group study rooms

Bottom right: Group study booths

Photography: Matt Wargo

Is there a college student who hasn't struggled with learning skills and teamwork? Recently, a donor reached out to help undergraduates at his alma mater through the new, one-floor, 7,000-square-foot David B. Weigle Information Commons designed by Ann Beha Architects, located in the Van Pelt-Dietrich Library Center, the main library of the University of Pennsylvania in Philadelphia. This state-of-the-art facility, including such group study spaces as private study rooms, café-style booths and flexible open space, a digital media laboratory and a 25-seat seminar room, reflects a profound change in fundamental academic values that is reshaping higher education throughout the nation. The Commons is an accessible, flexible and attractive learning environment where collaboration, skills development and new technology are part of everyday life. It transforms a once dark and uninviting space into a bright and dynamic one that rejects the traditional study carrel in favor of open spaces. The space also includes enclosed rooms that encourage groups large and small to work together, aided by expert advisers ready to help in critical reading and writing skills, presentation coaching and time/project management. The popularity of the Commons at this venerable Ivy League institution suggests it could be a prototype for other colleges and universities.

Ann Beha Architects

University of Pennsylvania
The Music Building Renovation and Addition
Philadelphia, Pennsylvania

"Penn Connects: A Vision For The Future," is a campus-wide effort to guide the University's growth over the next 30 years. The Music Building is an impressive example of this effort, with a three-story, 25,000-square-foot addition to the landmark Music Building, designed by Ann Beha Architects. The project restores the Italianate brick-and-terracotta exterior of the Music Building and adjacent Morgan Building, a pair of 1890 structures designed by Cope & Stewardson. The project also renovates the Music Building's interiors for administrative and faculty offices and building support spaces, and adds a new, terracotta-clad addition to accommodate acoustically sensitive functions, including practice rooms, recording studios, classrooms and faculty offices. While sympathetic to the Music Building, the addition reflects its own era with large expanses of glass, open circulation that incorporates the historic east façade. Open stairs, wide corridors and a new Music Terrace, connected to the new adjacent Campus Green, promote interaction and social activity inside and out. The project will also make history upon completion in 2009—as Penn's first LEED Silver certified building on campus.

Above left: First floor commons
Above center: Recital hall
Above right: Third floor commons
Left: Exterior at northeast corner
Illustration: Courtesy of Ann Beha Architects

17

Ann Beha Architects

Lafayette College
David Bishop Skillman Library Renovation and Expansion
Easton, Pennsylvania

Left: Exterior
Below left Gallery
Oppsoite: Skylighted atrium
Photography: Steven Wolfe

While a modern library stocked only with books seems inconceivable today, the David Bishop Skillman Library opened its doors in 1964 on the 340-acre campus of Lafayette College, in Easton, Pennsylvania, as mainly a repository for print materials and few spaces for readers or ancillary activities. Four decades later, Lafayette's main library reopened with a 75,000-square-foot renovation and three-level, 29,000-square-foot addition, designed by Ann Beha Architects, and is now one of the most important academic gathering places on campus. What transformed the previously undervalued and unappreciated brick Modernist structure? Its new form was driven by the college's desire for the main library to be a new resource for social interaction and intellectual discourse as well as a state-of-the-art college library. As a result, the new design provides a café, casual reading/ information meeting areas, group study areas, digital project rooms, gallery, special programs room, instruction rooms and computer laboratory along with the central book storage component, layering formal and casual program spaces along the north-south walk that organizes the building. Interestingly, because the original form of the library did not establish visual or physical connections with surrounding campus buildings, it lacked impact despite its prominent location on the main campus green. However, now that the new programmatic spaces are displayed to Lafayette's roughly 2,400 students through the largely transparent addition, and the revised massing of the building

Ann Beha Architects

aligns it with its neighbors and with campus circulation paths, the library is seen as a convenient and attractive place to work and socialize. Of course, it doesn't hurt that students are also attracted to the sleek, minimally detailed contemporary architecture and the spacious, well-lighted and handsomely tailored interiors. Such spaces as the open, skylighted "slot" between the original building and addition, which contain the primary circulation and stairs to all library functions, are exhilarating to experience on their own terms. Arthur J. Rothkopf, president of Lafayette, was not exaggerating at the rededication when he declared, "Skillman Library is the very heart of academic life at Lafayette. It is the leading symbol on our campus of Lafayette's commitment to academic excellence."

Top left: Periodical reading room

Left: Reading room

Anshen+Allen

901 Market Street, Suite 600 • San Francisco, CA 94103 • 415.281.5449 • (F) 415.882.9523

www.anshen.com

Anshen+Allen

University of Manchester
Sir Henry Wellcome Manchester Interdisciplinary Biocentre, John Garside Building
Manchester, United Kingdom

Formed in 2004 by the merger of two institutions that collaborated for over a century, the University of Manchester continues their tradition of distinguished research. (Ernest Rutherford began his pioneering work on atomic fission here.) For example, its Sir Henry Wellcome Manchester Interdisciplinary Biocentre - John Garside Building promotes interdisciplinary, challenge-oriented bioscience and biotechnology at the highest international level with the support of such facilities as its new, five-floor, 134,540-square-foot home, designed by Anshen+Allen. The facility comprises research laboratories, offices, meeting rooms, classrooms, dining, and core facilities. Its unique configuration begins with a state-of-the-art research block, wraps an office/meeting block around it, and inserts a five-story atrium between them. Sophisticated as its building technologies are, meeting such diverse goals as resisting vibration, lowering water consumption, conserving energy and providing flexibility in laboratory planning, the building also sustains a light, airy and stimulating setting for exchanging ideas. Thanks to a full spectrum of "interaction settings," from small meeting areas to seminar rooms, dining rooms and large lecture theaters, a public realm thrives among the laboratories and offices to celebrate the life sciences. John E.G. McCarthy, director of the Biocentre, declares, "The design is entirely successful in contributing to a collaborative environment."

Top left: Entrance with laboratory block on right, atrium in center and office block on left

Top right: Street elevation with public functions

Above: Seminar room

Opposite: Atrium

Photography: © Peter Cook/ VIEW (top left); © Daniel Hopkinson (top right, above and opposite)

Anshen+Allen

University of New Hampshire
College of Engineering and Physical Sciences, Kingsbury Hall
Durham, New Hampshire

A land-, sea-, and space-grant university, the University of New Hampshire encourages undergraduate and graduate students to pursue research with faculty mentors in regimes ranging from oceanic depths to outer space. On its 200-acre Durham campus, the university assiduously updates research facilities through remodeling and new construction. That's why students and faculty at the College of Engineering and Physical Sciences conduct interdisciplinary research and collaborative engineering in a state-of-the-art facility dating from 1950. A recent 80,000-square-foot renovation and 128,000-square-foot expansion, designed by Anshen+Allen, gives three-story-high Kingsbury Hall modern engineering teaching laboratories, classrooms, two-tiered lecture rooms, science library, student project space, machine shop, faculty offices, computer laboratories and lounge/café. Simultaneously, the new scheme creates a distinguished architectural presence on McDaniel Drive and College Road, while capturing north/south pedestrian movement. The building, following selective demolitions, insertions and façade modifications, includes a new main entry. Preserving the building's distinctive, function-oriented components, the makeover also adds a landscaped courtyard and paved courtyard where students can build and display projects. At the dedication, College dean Joseph Klewicki noted, "I know I speak for the entire CEPS faculty when I express my deep sense of gratitude for this wonderful building."

Above left: Tunnel experiments lab

Above right and opposite bottom left: Teaching laboratory

Right: New addition

Opposite bottom right: Exterior in evening view

Photography: © Anton Grassl/ Esto Photographics, Inc.

Anshen+Allen

University of Utah
College of Engineering, John E. and Marva M. Warnock Engineering Building
Salt Lake City, Utah

Below left: Alumni exhibition gallery

Below right: Informal student learning center

Below far right: Open stair

Bottom: Student plaza entry

Photography: © Cesar Rubio (bottom right); © Robert Canfield (below left, below right and below far right)

As Utah's economy expands and diversifies, the University of Utah's College of Engineering has been pivotal in helping the state meet workforce and technology needs. The College recently recorded an important milestone with the opening of the new, four-story, 100,000-square-foot John E. and Marva M. Warnock Engineering Building designed by Anshen+Allen in association with Prescott Muir Architects.

Besides providing the College a physical and intellectual hub, the new structure creates a coherent identity for the College, overcomes problems of site topography by reordering buildings and pedestrian corridors, and introduces such interactive spaces as the gallery that links the building's research and teaching components. Much space is dedicated to students, including classrooms, teaching laboratories,

computational facilities, auditorium classrooms, seminar rooms, group study rooms, informal study and meeting areas, and a café. But there are also such elements as the Dean's Suite (College administrative center) and Scientific Computing Institute for leading-edge work. "As the new face of engineering at the University of Utah," remarked College dean Richard Brown, "this building will be a place where the

engineers of tomorrow will be inspired to go out and change the world."

Anshen+Allen

University of California, Santa Cruz
Porter College Residence Halls
Santa Cruz, California

One of the more distinctive characteristics of the University of California, Santa Cruz is that all undergraduates living on campus or off are affiliated with its colleges. Students quickly learn that their colleges—Cowell, Stevenson, Crown, Merrill, Porter, Kresge, Oakes, Eight, Nine and Ten—resemble towns with residence quarters, faculty quarters, classrooms, dining facilities, marketplaces, and places of public assembly, while providing common academic bases for all first-year and transfer students. Designed by distinguished architects, the buildings span four decades of changing

tastes. The Residence Halls at Porter College, designed by Hugh Stubbins in 1968, are undergoing a renovation and expansion, designed by Anshen+Allen, to become modern 900-bed facilities. Along with seismic stabilization, "green" upgrades to conserve water, energy and other resources, full cladding replacement, and additions to floors to increase overall density, the interiors will be enhanced with new finishes, student lounge lanterns at corridor intersections, bathroom renovations, and carpet, window coverings and furniture. To preserve the spirit of the original archi-

tecture, the design calls for old and new construction to be clearly demarcated, new cladding to resemble the old, the mass of the expanded structure to be reduced, and the existing appearance of the courtyard to remain.

Above right: Elevator tower
Right: Student lounge lantern
Below: Exterior with courtyard
Illustration: Courtesy of Anshen+Allen

Cannon Design

Cannon Design

University of Maine
Student Recreation and Fitness Center
Orono, Maine

Established to teach "agriculture and mechanic arts," the University of Maine, in Orono, has offered students a strong, traditional and affordable education since 1862. Its enduring Yankee spirit is eloquently expressed in its largest building project to date, the two-story, 88,000-square-foot Student Recreation and Fitness Center, designed by Cannon Design. The Center directly supports the school's mission to create a more attractive campus with quality programs that enhance the learning environment. Some 1,500 visitors daily and over 13,000 intramural sports participants annually enjoy its fitness center, multi-purpose activity court, racquetball/squashball courts, natatorium, and three-court gymnasium with overhead jogging track. Yet the award-winning Center also makes connection—to nature and community—a primary theme in other ways. The copper, stone and glass-clad contemporary structure fits seamlessly into its wooded site, showcasing New England's natural beauty through ample fenestration, sustainable, locally harvested and manufactured materials, and highly efficient building systems, features that earned a LEED Silver certification. Equally important, the airy and open space, anchored by two double-height, skylighted circulation galleries, has become a mainstay of campus life, providing a venue for meetings, career fairs, open houses and community events as well as an irresistible gathering place for students, faculty and local residents.

Top left: South entry

Top right: Connecting stair and gallery

Right: Leisure/lap pool

Far right: Gymnasium

Opposite: Exterior view of weight training and fitness area

Photography: Anton Grassl/ Esto

California State University
Loker Student Union
Carson, California

It's no accident that the renovated and expanded Loker Student Union at California State University, Dominguez Hills, in Carson, designed by Cannon Design, is enticing more than 12,000 resident and commuting students to experience their school in a dramatically new way. The award-winning project updates the existing, 65,700-square-foot student union building and links it to a 71,500-square-foot addition via a new, multi-level courtyard that serves as a symbolic campus core. Consequently, the expanded student union projects a fresh, inviting and boldly contemporary image for such renovated and new facilities as the fine dining restaurant, food court and sports bar, lounge and study areas, bookstore, office space for student organizations and student government, conference rooms and 500-seat ballroom. Not only are interiors enhanced by abundant daylight and outdoor views, generous sightlines that display what is happening in multiple areas, and attractive furnishings that encourage informality, relaxation and socializing, they constitute a meaningful conservation of construction materials. More than 50 percent of the existing mechanical, electrical and plumbing infrastructure has been reused in the completed project. For all these reasons and more, *American School and University* hailed the project as "Well-detailed inside and out. A very impactful renovation and addition."

Right: Informal lounge
Below left: Main entry
Bottom right: Exterior
Opposite: Informal lounge area flanking main entrance
Photography: Assissi Productions

Cannon Design

Plymouth State University
Langdon Woods Residence Hall
Plymouth, New Hampshire

To combat community discontent with student competition for rental properties and to attract upperclassmen back to campus housing with contemporary accommodations that offered greater privacy, variety and amenities, Plymouth State University, a component of the University System of New Hampshire in Plymouth, recently unveiled the new, 347-bed, five-story, 114,000-square-foot Langdon Woods Residence Hall, designed by Cannon Design, to appeal to upperclassmen by promoting individual development, campus life and green design principles. The new brick and glass-clad, LEED Gold-certified facility has been developed for just this purpose with two components, the 218-bed Sophomore Building to the south, offering double rooms, each with a bathroom, and the 129-bed Junior/Senior Building to the north, equipped with four-person suites, each with four single bedrooms, furnished common area and bathroom. Resembling a microcosm of society, with a multipurpose room, computer cluster, lounge seating, wireless internet, café, kitchen, fitness room, laundry, bicycle storage and residence life offices on the ground floor, and double-height lounge spaces on residential floors, it continually fosters interaction and collaboration among students and staff. Commenting on the project's nurturing environment and use of sustainable materials and green building systems, Plymouth's President Sara Jayne Steen recently proclaimed, "We are developing our students' life skills as they learn to live in an environmentally sustainable community."

Top left: Multi-purpose room
Top right: South entry
Upper left: Southwest elevation
Left: Café and lounge
Lower left: Double room
Photography: Anton Grassl/ Esto

Cannon Design

University of Kansas Medical Center
Kansas Life Sciences Innovation Center
Kansas City, Kansas

Architecture's power to shape landscape as well as interior space is dramatized by the five-story, 202,500-square-foot Kansas Life Sciences Innovation Center at the University of Kansas Medical Center. Designed by Cannon Design, the facility is envisioned as a new center of research for the university's expanding medical campus, where academic units operate alongside the University of Kansas Hospital. The Innovation Center reflects the University's commitment to innovative life science research through advanced facilities for a wide range of disciplines. Its red-sandstone-and-brick exterior acts as a new gateway to the campus beyond, anticipating future development from its perch at the edge of a plateau. On its north side, laboratories with expansive windows enjoy vistas of city and prairie. To the south, office suites overlook the campus. While laboratories are efficient and modular to permit flexible assignment of research teams, "neighbor-hoods" of laboratory offices, breakout spaces and labora-tory suites create dynamic settings for multi-disciplinary teaming. The core is equally purposeful, accommodating building systems and support functions while encouraging interaction along encircling circulation paths. Yet at night, the building's light creates a magic interplay between man and nature on the prairie.

Right, in descending order: Exterior at southwest corner, lobby, typical laboratory, stairwell looking onto lobby

Below left: View from major thoroughfare

Photography: Richard Pettis Photography

Cannon Design

University System of Maryland Universities at Shady Grove Camille Kendall Academic Center
Rockville, Maryland

Conceived as a "speculative university building," the new, five-story, 195,000-square-foot Camille Kendall Academic Center at the Universities at Shady Grove, part of the University System of Maryland, brings a different kind of facility to the USG campus in Rockville. The Center has been designed by Cannon Design to provide educational programs and opportunities to people associated with the local biomedical industry. Its three-part structure, consisting of office, classroom and support components, is simultaneously sophisticated, flexible and generic enough to accommodate future changes driven by technology and curriculum, yet adheres to sustainable design principles so rigorously that it earned LEED Gold certification. To fulfill its demanding mission, the Center immerses its classrooms, laboratories, library, administrative and support offices, bookstore, food service/dining, fitness center, lounges and faculty offices in a rich mix of public and private spaces for work, gathering and circulation. Its details are telling. For example, column spacing and ceiling heights in teaching spaces can accept at least four configurations representing distinct teaching methods and pedagogies. In addition, laboratory spaces can satisfy a wide spectrum of research types, and classrooms are convertible to laboratories. No wonder the Center was AIA Maryland's "Public Building of the Year" for 2007.

Top left: South office wing
Top right: Student and staff lounge
Above: Learning resource center
Right: Atrium
Photography: Bjorg Magnea

CO Architects

5055 Wilshire Blvd., 9th Floor • Los Angeles, CA 90036 • 323.525.0500 • (F) 323.525.0955

www.coarchitects.com

CO Architects

University of Wisconsin-Madison
Microbial Sciences Building
Madison, Wisconsin

New construction can help schools resolve old challenges in creative ways, and the versatile Microbial Sciences Building at the University of Wisconsin-Madison illustrates why. The six-floor, 330,000-square-foot, brick-clad structure, designed by CO Architects as design architect and Plunkett Raysich Architects as architect of record, convenes microbiologists from three core microbial sciences departments on campus, including bacteriology, food microbiology and toxicology, and medical microbiology and immunology. Housing them under one roof establishes a stimulating work environment where faculty and students have access to a 450-seat symposium center, discovery center and sophisticated classrooms in addition to modern teaching laboratories and neighborhoods of secure research laboratories, support space and investigator offices. In addition, the building courts the larger campus population through such features as a public "street," rising with the grade from the northwest corner to the southeast corner. Public functions on the first two levels add vitality to the "street," encouraging general use. To facilitate interaction, the interiors surround two dramatic atria equipped with strategically placed meeting places, cafés and open seating, including the larger atrium to the south and smaller atrium to the east. The result is a unique setting where both microbiologists and the campus community are welcome.

Above: Exterior at southwest with heritage oak tree

Top right: Exterior displaying north atrium

Above right: North atrium

Right: Seating on atrium floor

Opposite: Fourth floor view of atrium

Photography: Assassi Productions

CO Architects

University of Washington
William H. Foege Building
Seattle, Washington

Founded in 1861, Seattle-based University of Washington, one of the world's preeminent research universities, recently advanced its biomedical research with state-of-the-art facilities for genome sciences and bioengineering. Interestingly, the new five-floor, 296,000-square-foot William H. Foege Building, designed by CO Architects, also demonstrates the complex site requirements imposed on contemporary architecture. Not only does the structure create two separate yet linked facilities—integrated research space for bioengineering's team and individual research activities plus flexible laboratory lofts for genome sciences' wet and computational research—it defines a campus boundary descending to Portage Bay. On its westerly façade, terracotta tile continues the traditional brick campus. However, on its easterly façade, a glass-and-metal skin adds sparkle and movement to the new quadrangle fronting the Health Sciences Campus. To foster encounters between researchers and draw university people though the building, an internal circulation spine connects three levels and descends 45 feet from the campus to the bay. Entries, lounges, reading spaces and an atrium animate this internal street, leading to a café with a waterfront terrace. Noting how the design mirrors UW's collaborative spirit, university president Mark Emmert said, "This building is, of course, a wonderful exemplar of what the UW is all about."

Above: Exterior from Portage Bay

Right: Stairs along internal street

Far right: Curtainwall detail

Opposite top: Lounge

Opposite bottom, left and right: Sunscreens, easterly façade

Photography: Lara Swimmer Photography

41

CO Architects

Texas Tech University Health Sciences Center, El Paso
Paul L. Foster School of Medicine, Medical Education Building
El Paso, Texas

One of three cornerstone buildings planned for the new, Paul L. Foster School of Medicine, part of the seven campus Texas Tech University Health Sciences Center, the new, five-story, 125,000-square-foot Medical Education Building expands TTU's existing graduate program in El Paso to a full, four-year medical school. Its stately, brick-and-limestone structure, designed by CO Architects in the university's Spanish Renaissance style, helps the School alleviate a severe shortage of physicians in the region. In addition, the design supports a new medical curriculum that emphasizes small-group,

problem-based learning and integrates clinical training in the first two years. Accordingly, it incorporates basic science laboratories, such core teaching spaces as small-group learning rooms, case method classrooms and two 100-seat lecture halls, 50-seat computer-based testing laboratoray, clinical skills trainging and medical simulation space, library, along with faculty and administrative offices, student lounges, wellness center and café. Located a few blocks from TTU's existing El Paso facilities, the building anchors the north end of the campus, focusing on an intimate, internal courtyard that serves as an outdoor living room for students and faculty. A sign of its importance is its understated yet visible role as a primary campus entrance, signified by its major entryway and vertical tower.

Top: Stairwell

Above: Lecture hall

Left: Café

Far left: Second-floor terrace

Below: Courtyard and medicinal garden

Photography: Robert Canfield Photography

CO Architects

University of California, Los Angeles
Engineering V
Los Angeles, California

Engineering V exemplifies the multi-purpose facilities that are indispensable to research institutions such as the University of California, Los Angeles. Designed by CO Architects to give UCLA flexibility to accommodate wide-ranging engineering research methodologies, the five-floor, 120,000-square-foot, brick-and-terracotta-clad concrete structure houses material sciences laboratories and a new bioengineering program for cutting-edge research. It represents the first phase of a three-phase development replacing two 1950s buildings, and occupies a transitional zone between the original core campus to the northeast and the newer healthcare campus to the south. Despite its flexibility, the building establishes a genuine sense of place through its well-defined organization. For example, non-technical spaces form the northern entry façade facing Portola Walk, a major campus pedestrian walk, and are reached from an internal east-west circulation spine lined with student breakout areas, lounges and open stairways that encourage social interaction. Engineering 5 connects to the campus at three levels. While the main entry faces north, where the third floor is on grade, the first floor faces south onto the service alley, where the site drops 35 feet, and the fourth level connects to the adjacent engineering building via a suspended bridge—adding a glimmer of flair to exceptional utility.

Above left: Stairway

Left: Classroom

Below left: Main entrance at north façade

Below: Suspended bridge

Photography: Robert Canfield Photography

Derck & Edson Associates

Derck & Edson Associates

Bloomsburg University of Pennsylvania
Academic Quad
Bloomsburg, Pennsylvania

To upgrade the quality of campus life, many of the nation's schools are reclaiming the heart of their real estate from automobiles, pushing roads and parking to the periphery in favor of open space and pedestrian walkways. The benefits from this new approach to planning are highly visible at the new Academic Quadrangle of Bloomsburg University of Pennsylvania, in Bloomsburg, Pennsylvania. The 150,000-square-foot "quad," designed by landscape architect Derck & Edson Associates, provides a central area for circulation and assembly to serve everything from chance encounters to graduation ceremonies for 7,000 attendees. To accommodate this large expanse, the project team relocated a sizable parking lot, incorporated an historic fountain and existing art/sculptures, provided emergency access to all surrounding buildings, maintained visual sight lines to the library, and circumvented or repositioned utilities. Since the design solution represents a comprehensive look at the environment, materials reflect the historic Bloomsburg aesthetic, larger shade trees provide shade and reduce the heat island effect, added green spaces alleviate run off, and accent lighting enhances public safety by illuminating building facades and art/sculptures. Not surprisingly, Bloomburg's 27,000 students have wasted no time turning the green center of their 280-acre campus into a favored gathering place.

Top left: Casual seating area
Top right: Aerial view
Left: Fountain plaza
Right: Walkway
Opposite top: Previous site conditions
Photography: Nathan Cox

Derck & Edson Associates

Alvernia University
Campus Commons
Reading, Pennsylvania

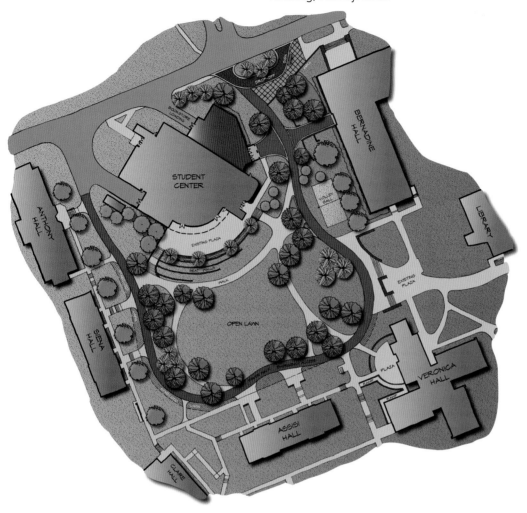

Although Alvernia University has grown impressively since its founding as a teachers' seminarium in 1926 by the Bernardine Sisters, a Franciscan Order of the Catholic Church, it never had a central green space—until the arrival of the new 78,000-square-foot Campus Commons, designed by landscape architect Derck & Edson Associates. The project site was already occupied by a busy parking lot. However, its location was ideal, adjacent to the Student Union and surrounded by residential buildings serving the more than 2,800 men and women studying at the four-year liberal arts college. Accordingly, the designers relocated the parking lot, connected the various destination points encircling the space with walkways, and made room for emergency vehicles as well as passenger vehicles moving students in and out during the school year. (The main perimeter concrete walk is 12 feet wide with an additional 12 feet of grass pavers along the outer edge to handle fire trucks.) The new Commons makes good use of its grass pavers, brick and concrete to create beautiful and functional spaces. For casual recreation such as sunbathing and Frisbee and such organized events as band concerts, barbecues and large tent gatherings, the Commons is now the "in" place to be outdoors.

Above left: Site plan

Above right: Overall view

Opposite right, far right: Previous site condition, players in pick-up game

Opposite lower right, far right: Renderings of walkways

Photography: Steve Woit (players); Associated Construction (all others)

Illustration: Courtesy of Derck & Edson Associates

Derck & Edson Associates

Susquehanna University
West Village Housing
Selinsgrove, Pennsylvania

Perceived as detached from the rest of the buildings on the 306-acre campus of Susquehanna University, in Selinsgrove, Pennsylvania, West Hall will soon become the center of a little enclave to be called West Village Housing. Working with the housing architect and university officials, landscape architect Derck & Edson Associates has designed landscaping appropriate for a phased project that will be constructed two buildings at a time towards a total of seven. The LEED-certified design supports the concept of residences whose front porches line a pedestrian spine, creating the intimate feel of a village. At the same time, it addresses numerous other practical concerns. Besides providing access to daily service vehicles, emergency services, and student move ins and move outs, the landscaping works around existing geothermal fields, keeps buildings above the adjacent stream and associated flood plains, conforms to the requirements of a sustainable site that causes minimal environmental disturbance, uses plant material without need of permanent irrigation, and preserves over 60 percent of the site as open space. Praising the design's high quality, Michael A. Coyne, vice president for finance and treasurer of Susquehanna University, recently declared, "Experience has taught us we can count on Derck & Edson Associates."

Below and above right: West Hall and circular path

Right: Tree-lined pedestrian spine

Opposite above: Site plan

Photography: Nathan Cox

Illustration: Courtesy of Derck & Edson Associates

WEST HALL

DEGENSTEIN CAMPUS CENTER

AIKENS HALL

Derck & Edson Associates

Birmingham-Southern College
Urban Environmental Park
Birmingham, Alabama

The last link in a chain of open spaces at Birmingham-Southern College, a four-year, liberal arts institution founded in 1856 and affiliated with the United Methodist Church, the upcoming, 13-acre Urban Environmental Park and its new lake, informal amphitheater and lakeside plaza, designed by Derck & Edson Associates, will be a shady, green and refreshing retreat from the more densely developed portions of the school's 192-acre campus, three miles west of downtown Birmingham, Alabama. Along with drawing together circulation paths from the intramural fields, nearby eco-garden, future student activities building and lakeside amenities, the park will become a true campus destination. Its proximity to neighboring student residences will attract students seeking to relax, study and socialize. Yet it will also serve as an educational resource by offering first-hand lessons on environmental issues. For example, the lake and its attending open spaces deliberately incorporate the site's existing mature trees, the low-lying area will be enhanced with water-loving plants to help naturally recharge storm water runoff, and the lake fringe is nurturing desirable wildlife by using native and naturalized plant materials. Will the park also achieve its goal of feeling like a mature landscape from day one? That's the plan.

Top left: Aerial view

Top right: Site plans

Above left: Lakeside plaza

Left: Informal amphitheater

Illustration: Courtesy of Derck & Edson Associates

DiMella Shaffer

281 Summer Street • Boston, MA 02210 • 617.426.5004 • (F) 617.426.0046
1511 Third Avenue, Suite 300 • Seattle, WA 98101 • 206.686.0170 • (F) 206.686.0171
www.dimellashaffer.com

DiMella Shaffer

North Shore Community College
Berry Academic Building
Danvers, Massachusetts

Of 15 community colleges in Massachusetts, North Shore Community College is one of the oldest and largest, founded in 1965 and serving some 7,500 students annually on campuses in Lynn, Beverly and Danvers. Like other community colleges, North Shore takes a progressive view of its mission. When the Danvers campus needed to expand beyond its converted manufacturing facility, it raised its profile dramatically by developing the three-story, 106,000 square foot Berry Academic Building, designed by DiMella Shaffer. The award-winning facility, housing classrooms, library, administrative and faculty offices, cafeteria and student support services, opens a new front door to the campus through dynamic contrasts. Its two wings are bisected by a monolithic, three-story, cast stone wall that meets each wing at different angles. Not only does the more colorful and active classroom wing clearly differ from the more formal services wing, which holds the cafeteria, library and offices, the central circulation spine is enlivened by two-story spaces and glass-enclosed stairwells promoting visibility at all levels. Wayne Burton, President of the College, praises the project as, "One of the best-designed public buildings in Massachusetts."

Top right: Light filled lounge

Right: Arcade at entrance

Far right: Cantilevered stairwell at cast stone wall

Photography: Richard Mandelkorn

DiMella Shaffer

University of New Hampshire
Gables Residence Hall
Durham, New Hampshire

Left, bottom and right:
Exterior of South buildings,
North building gateway, new
recreational quadrangle

Far left, below: Ground floor
public spaces and study alcoves

Photography: Richard
Mandelkorn

56

To house more of the 13,000 University of New Hampshire students who enjoy studying amid the rolling hills and riverbeds of the 200-acre Durham campus, the recent expansion of the Gables Residence Hall enhances the sense of community and diminishes the sense of isolation and distance to the main campus. Two new six- and seven-story-high buildings, designed by DiMella Shaffer, add 400 beds and 160,000 square feet to the complex. Besides providing appealing apartments and student amenities, the award-winning design successfully resolves the larger planning issues. The two brick, copper and slate-clad structures provide the Gables a North and South gateway, drawing campus pedestrians through its outdoor spaces, forming a new quadrangle to support student recreational activities. Their interiors are equally impressive. Nine to ten suites form well-defined communities of 50 residents per floor. To help students connect, there are also study lounges on each floor that command beautiful outdoor views, as well as connect student areas for social activities. Commending DiMella Shaffer on its work, Dana Peterson, AIA, Associate University Architect, shared, "They are unparalleled in their ability to come up with creative solutions."

DiMella Shaffer

Bridgewater State College
Crimson Hall
Bridgewater, Massachusetts

College President Dana Mohler-Faria calls Crimson Hall "the crown jewel of residence halls in Massachusetts." Bridgewater State College's new residence hall, in Bridgewater, Massachusetts, designed by DiMella Shaffer, shows how resident hall design can enhance campus planning as well as student life. The main problem facing the project stemmed from the site. A commuter railroad divides the College's 235-acre campus into east and west halves linked by a pedestrian path traversing parking lots on both sides of the tracks. The College wanted Crimson Hall, a 408-bed, four-and five-story, 137,000 square foot facility, to create an assuring new identity for the East Campus along with desirable residences. Accordingly, the brick-clad facility joins the existing DiNardo Hall to form an inviting quadrangle that acts as the East Campus's new "landing pad," reached by a substantial reconfigured pathway. Indoors, the glass bridge houses large lounges and community kitchens on all floors, establishing natural gathering places for study, dining, recreation and meetings. In addition, the four- and six-bed suites are comfortably furnished, and common elements are conveniently placed on the ground floors of both wings, including the entrance lobby, recreation and study rooms, laundry, multi-use conference center and 270-seat dining room.

DiMella Shaffer

Cape Cod Community College
Lyndon P. Lorusso Applied Technology Building
West Barnstable, Massachusetts

Located on Cape Cod, where environmental challenges have for years included water quality, smart growth, reliable energy sources, natural resources and transportation, Cape Cod Community College has been a long-time advocate of sustainable design. How appropriate, therefore, that the College's new, three-floor, 27,000 square foot Lyndon P. Lorusso Applied Technology Building, a 408-bed, four-and five-story, 137,000 square foot facility, designed by DiMella Shaffer is to be Massachusetts's first state-funded LEED-certified "green" building as well as a state-of-the-art facility for teaching technology. The design is replete with sustainable elements, such as a rainwater collection and re-use system, rooftop and sunshade solar panel PV system, water-efficient plumbing fixtures and regional building materials. Yet the brick-clad structure is also an outstanding learning environment, placing classrooms, open computer laboratory, work force training, student/faculty lounge and network operations center in spacious, naturally illuminated and attractive settings. One space even attracts visitors from the entire school. Because the monumental steps scaling the sloping site split the building in two, a second-floor glass bridge spans the divide-and the student/faculty lounge it supports is one of the College's most popular meeting places. For this and other reasons, College President Kathleen Schatzberg calls the building "a showpiece for the College, Division of Capital Asset Management and all partners involved."

Top: Glass enclosed stair

Above: Second floor glass bridge above monumental stair

Left and right: Views of student/faculty lounge

Photography: Richard Mandelkorn

Earl Swensson Associates, Inc. (ESa)

ESa

Belmont University
Gordon E. Inman Center,
College of Health Sciences & Nursing
Nashville, Tennessee

On 75 historic acres of the former Belle Monte estate, two miles southwest of downtown Nashville, Belmont University has thrived since 1890 as one of America's fastest growing Christian universities, now enrolling over 5,000 students. Besides earning such distinctions as *U.S. News & World Report*'s Top 15 regional ranking in the "Best Universities—Masters" category, the school recently completed the new, four-story, 71,000-square-foot Gordon E. Inman Center, designed by ESa, to consolidate programs of the College of Health Sciences & Nursing. Since the structure required spatial and technological flexibility for present and future needs, responsiveness is visibly expressed throughout its classrooms, laboratories, administrative offices and conference facilities. Thus, instructional spaces provide realistic healthcare settings, laboratories simulate a wide range of specialized environments, and classrooms offer state-of-the-art AV packages. For all its sophistication, the Center is also a good citizen to its neighbors. Not only does its Neoclassical-Italianate architecture reaffirm the "uniquely Belmont" blend of warmth, hospitality and tradition, its top floor conference center invites community use. And because the Center supports a new nursing education model that addresses the nation's shortage of nurses, HCA/Tri-Star has chosen Belmont to form relationships with other higher-education institutions in a regional Nursing Consortium.

Above: Exterior
Below: Boardroom
Far right: Central lobby
Opposite upper left: Musculo-skeletal learning space
Opposite upper right: Boardroom lounge
Photography: Scott McDonald/ Hedrich Blessing

ESa

Right: Auditorium facing proscenium

Bottom left: Black box theater

Bottom right: Main lobby

Opposite: Exterior

Photography: © Vince Wallace/ Silverhill Images

Belmont University
Bill and Carole Troutt Theater
Nashville, Tennessee

Parishioners no longer worship in the original sanctuary of Nashville's Belmont Heights Baptist Church, which opened on prominent Belmont Boulevard in 1920, but the handsome brick-and-stone edifice remains as vital as ever. Reborn as Belmont University's Bill and Carole Troutt Theater, a 37,110-square-foot renovation, conversion and expansion designed by ESa, it serves local professional theater and dance companies as well as Belmont's Department of Theater and Dance. The 357-seat auditorium (featuring raked floor seating, proscenium arch and fly tower), main lobby, scene shop and black box theater were creatively fashioned from the former church at the architect's suggestion, giving the structure new life after offices of the School of Nursing departed. While much of the already altered interior was gutted, original documents permitted the building's essence, including original moldings, doors and window casings, to be replicated. In addition, such hidden treasures as the sanctuary's original barrel vaulted ceiling reemerged to take their place in the new scheme, bestowing authenticity and sense of place. The award-winning renovation even improves the original building's design, replacing steep monumental steps to the main level with gentler, curving twin staircases and revealing the lower level's new main lobby and box office.

ESa

Brentwood Academy
Rodgers-Dale Performing Arts Center
Brentwood, Tennessee

To nurture and challenge each whole person—body, mind, and spirit—to the glory of God has been the mission of Brentwood Academy since 1970, an independent Christian school in Brentwood, Tennessee for grades 6-12. How broadly the Academy views its mission is impressively demonstrated by its new, two-level, 28,627-square-foot Fine Arts Center, designed by ESa to house instrumental and vocal music, dance and theater arts. The award-winning structure combines practicality and vision. A 2,500-square-foot black box experimental theater, dance studio, chorus room, classrooms, office space and lobby occupy the entry level, complemented by a band room, private practice rooms, sectional rehearsal rooms and forensics classroom on the lower level, with a proscenium theater connected

to the lobby envisioned as a future addition. Meanwhile, flexible accommodations help maximize the facility's utility. The 150-seat black box theater, for example, can readily transform itself into a recording studio, rehearsal space, theater for one-act plays, forensics rehearsal space, performance room for cheerleader practice and dance instruction, or meeting/seminar space. Nineteen feet above its floor, a wire mesh tension grid replaces traditional catwalks to let aspiring theater technicians operate theater productions more safely—showing students how even the humblest details can enrich everyday life.

Top: Exterior
Above left: Band room
Left: Dance studio
Opposite: Corridor Gallery
Photography: © Vince Wallace/ Silverhill Images

ESa

Belmont University
Maple Hall
Nashville, Tennessee

How is Nashville's Belmont University coping with a rising enrollment that now exceeds 5,000 students, a 60 percent increase since 2000? Like many other growing colleges and universities, the highly rated Christian school is building new student housing. Students of the Class of 2012 arrived on the 75-acre campus in August 2008 to discover a newly finished freshman residence hall, a six-story, 49,475-square-foot brick-and-limestone structure designed by ESa. The first of three such halls that will group freshman along a new, centrally located campus mall, the facility houses 198 students on separate floors for men and women. Its design supports freshman life in more ways than one. Living units encourage community, with floors two through five each having 19 double rooms, each sharing a bath with an adjoining room, the first floor hosting 13 doubles, and the sixth floor adding a commons lounge area and two triple rooms. Interior materials and finishes such as natural, PVC-free dolomite composition tile in dormitory rooms and baths, recyclable carpet tile and backing covering corridors and seating areas, and "eco-balance" marmoleum flooring in the main lobby and elevator lobbies complement the floor plans, making the environment as healthy as it is friendly.

Elkus Manfredi Architects

300 A Street • Boston, MA 02210 • 617.426.1300 • (F) 617.426.7502

www.elkus-manfredi.com

Elkus Manfredi Architects

Harvard University
Graduate Commons
Cambridge, Massachusetts

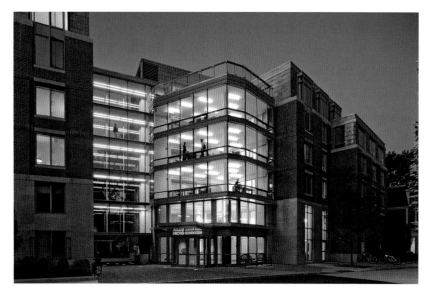

Harvard University Graduate Commons represents an ambitious plan to add graduate housing on campus and to transform the edge of the University's campus at the Riverside neighborhood in Cambridge, Massachusetts. The irregular surface parking lots required different urban design solutions to both allow density and to reinforce the residential character of the neighborhood through careful infill and building relocation. The central element of the project is a new six-story residence hall with 141 apartments on Cowperthwaite Street, with 190 parking and 75 bicycle spaces on three levels below-grade. To maintain the permeability of the block, and to mediate between the scale of Harvard's adjacent dormitory towers and the adjacent pedestrian-scaled neighborhood, the building is carefully manipulated in massing and height to fit comfortably within its context. The residences feature significant opportunities for planned and unplanned interaction: a multi-function common room, dining room, and roof deck, plus laundry facilities and study rooms. The façades are clad in brick, copper, limestone, and granite — materials that closely relate to the vernacular of Harvard's historic residential buildings. The building has received a LEED Gold rating.

Above left: Evening view

Above right: Exterior at street level

Right: Residence hall and new infill woodframe residence

Below right: Sixth-floor terrace

Opposite: View overlooking Cowperthwaite Street

Photography: Robert Benson

Elkus Manfredi Architects

The Ohio State University
South Campus Gateway
Columbus, Ohio

Left: Intersection of High and
11th Streets

Above: Evening scene with OSU
students

Lower left: Apartments

Bottom left: Office building
housing university bookstore

Opposite: Cinema entrance on
pedestrian plaza

Photography: Brad Feinknopf,
Eric Wagner

In order to reinvent its "front door" and to create a precinct of common amenities for students and the adjacent neighborhood, The Ohio State University has initiated the rehabilitation of High Street — transforming a physical barrier into a seam with the community. South Campus Gateway is the first phase of development. Students, faculty, neighbors, and visitors mingle in a lively environment that includes extensive retail at street level, 12 restaurants, an eight-screen cinema, 184 residential units, and the University bookstore, moved off-campus to draw neighbors as well as students. Constant pedestrian activity unites the University and its surroundings in an inviting college town atmosphere. In turn, the project has made the University's cultural resources more accessible to the City of Columbus, creating incentive for junior faculty and others to live in adjacent residential neighborhoods. This synergy between University and city has encouraged a more livable community around the University, generated by the Gateway transformation.

Elkus Manfredi Architects

Boston University
School of Hospitality Administration
Boston, Massachusetts

Every detail of Boston University's three-floor, 30,000-square-foot School of Hospitality Administration is focused on preparing students for the business of managing hotels, food service, travel and tourism, and entertainment. In renovating the existing building, the design team's goal was to create spaces which were conducive to learning, and also to bring the hotel into the school in order to simulate the true hospitality environments that students encounter upon graduation. The program included a food preparation kitchen, labs, classrooms, an information and resource center, reception and lounge areas, an auditorium, a computer laboratory, the Dean's suite, a boardroom, and student/faculty and alumni facilities. Elkus Manfredi's designers moved the obstructive, centrally-located egress stair to one side of the building's narrow footprint, establishing an off-center circulation axis that opened the entry area to public gathering spaces, all of which are placed on the ground floor. Student and classroom areas are housed on the second floor, with faculty facilities on the third. Clean, contemporary lines, good lighting, and a natural, neutral palette of wood paneling, floor-to-ceiling glass, and stone flooring are accented with colorful furniture, imparting an overall sense of quality that achieves the Dean's stated goal that the building be designed "with the school's international reputation in mind."

Above: Information and resource center

Far left: Classroom and corridor

Left: Boardroom

Lower far left: Auditorium

Lower left: Dean's suite

Opposite: Reception

Photography: © Bruce T. Martin, all rights reserved

Elkus Manfredi Architects

Emerson College
The Paramount Center
Boston, Massachusetts

The newest addition to Emerson College's downtown Boston expansion, the mixed-use Paramount Center strengthens Emerson's highly specialized curricula in communication and the arts. Located in the heart of Boston's Theatre District, the Center was built on the site of the existing Paramount Theater and neighboring 545 Washington Street building, plus an adjacent vacant lot. Elkus Manfredi's designers undertook redevelopment of the existing theater and the design of 154,000 square feet of new construction. The granite façade of an 1860s structure on the constricted site was preserved and incorporated into the new design. Emerson's ambitious program included conversion of the Paramount Theater, formerly a 1,500-seat cinema, to a 590-seat proscenium lyrical theater for staged productions. Furniture was reupholstered in original Art Deco style; chromo-chronology testing of surviving paint samples permitted recreation of the original color palette. Other program elements include a black box theater, a scene shop and loading dock, rehearsal and dance studios, a soundstage, practice rooms, dressing rooms, classrooms, faculty offices, a student lounge/assembly space and cafè, a 180-seat film screening room, a 150-seat restaurant, and dormitory housing for 262 students. The Paramount Center was declared by Mayor Thomas Menino to be "a new chapter in Boston's cultural history."

Above left: Main elevation on Washington Street

Above right: Perspective on Mason Street Place

Right: Black box theater

Below: Section through 590-seat lyrical theater

Illustration: Courtesy of Elkus Manfredi Architects

ELS Architecture and Urban Design

ELS Architecture and Urban Design

Berkeley High School
Student Union and Recreation Center
Berkeley, California

The only public high school in Berkeley, California, Berkeley High School is a vibrant academic community whose 3,000 students represent diverse racial, ethnic and socioeconomic backgrounds and consistently graduate to two- and four-year colleges and universities. The campus of Art Deco buildings enjoys similar distinction, being included in the National Register of Historic Places. Facing Berkeley's Civic Center Historic District on its north side, the new, two-story student union and recreation center, designed by ELS Architecture and Urban Design, maintains the school's architectural tradition, supports the social mission of the school, and enlivens the campus. The award-winning architecture contrasts cast-in-place concrete with transparent window walls to relate to the 1930s-era campus, welcome participation and reconnect the school to the community. The 86,250-square-foot building includes a library, cafeteria, performance space, classrooms, career counseling and administrative offices, all in an open, inviting environment that flows naturally through a glazed lobby into the recreation center's gymnasium, natatorium and dance studios. Glass walls between the gymnasium and dining area slide open to accommodate school-wide and community events. The project was honored with the President's Award from the Downtown Berkeley Association for giving the students and the community new pride and ownership in their surroundings. Vandalism and graffiti have noticeably decreased. "The whole campus has changed as has the way the community views the school," says Jack McLaughlin, superintendent of Berkeley Public Schools at the time of construction. "What a difference a building can make!"

Below: Breezeway and student union

Right: Student union

Opposite top, left to right: Street entrance, library and gymnasium in recreation center

Photography: Timothy Hursley, David Wakely (gymnasium)

ELS Architecture and Urban Design

Cragmont Elementary School
Berkeley, California

Replacing a seismically unsafe structure, the new Cragmont Elementary School in Berkeley is designed by ELS Architecture and Urban Design to utilize the surrounding environment as an extension of the classroom and to blend in with the Arts and Crafts architecture of the Berkeley Hills neighborhood. The design enhances learning by connecting students to the landscape with a rooftop terrace, outdoor play areas, a garden, classrooms with large windows and balconies, and ground floor classrooms

that open to outdoor patios. The 450-student body raised standardized test scores by 38 percentile points one year after moving in from the previous location where they had been temporarily housed for a decade. Fitting harmoniously into its residential neighborhood, the award-winning, 45,000-square-foot school is also a very good neighbor, thanks to its compatible scale, massing, materials, finishes and colors. The school's careful positioning against a steep hillside, previously thought unbuildable, preserves bay views for adjacent homes and maximizes usable space for outdoor learning and recreation activities. The successful program and design were developed with parents, teachers, administrators, students, and neighbors in an intensive series of workshops. The interiors, comprising 21 classrooms, library, multi-purpose room, and administration/human resources offices, are designed with the community in mind. Classrooms are clustered in groups of three along two wings, while common spaces are adjacent and open to a central plaza, enabling the school to double as a community center, neighborhood gathering place and, in the event of an earthquake, emergency relief shelter.

Above: View from playing fields and multi-purpose room
Left: Rooftop terrace
Opposite: Library
Lower left: Main entrance
Photography: Timothy Hursley

ELS Architecture and Urban Design

First Presbyterian Church of Berkeley
Christian Education Center
Berkeley, California

First Presbyterian Church of Berkeley was founded one day before the city of Berkeley was incorporated on March 31, 1878. Growing up with its city and famous neighbor, the University of California, Berkeley, First Presbyterian continues to maintain a deep commitment to Christian education as a major component of its ministry. In order to accommodate its growing congregation, the Church retained ELS Architecture and Urban Design to develop a new, three-story education building – named Geneva Hall – that houses classrooms, meeting rooms, a small chapel, and a student cafe/lounge, as well as renovate the historic 1906 McKinley Hall, which had fallen into disuse after being converted first to World War II housing and later to student housing. With the Geneva Hall addition to the three existing church buildings, ELS's design team was faced with the challenge of maintaining the feeling of a campus. The solution involved designing the new education building in an L-shape to create a plaza and rotating McKinley Hall 180 degrees over two levels of new underground parking to face the new plaza. Spared from being demolished, the 9,300-square-foot McKinley Hall has been returned to its original use as a school building with its exterior restored and interior converted back into educational and office space. The 120,000-square-foot project incorporates abundant daylighting, passive cooling and heating techniques, and energy-efficient systems. First Presbyterian now has 70 percent more classroom and meeting space, 10 percent more staff space, and a safe learning environment welcoming people from all walks of life.

Top: Geneva Hall and central plaza

Left top to bottom: Music rehearsal room, cafe/lounge, library/conference room and McKinley Hall

Photography: David Wakely, Treve Johnson (McKinley Hall)

ELS Architecture and Urban Design

Fresno City College
Historic Old Administrative Building
Fresno, California

Left: Historic aerial view

Lower left: New auditorium

Bottom left: New floor plan

Illustration: Courtesy of ELS Architecture and Urban Design

Aerial Photography: Courtesy of Fresno City College

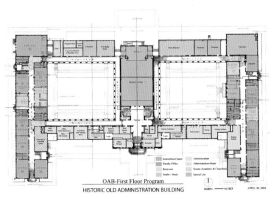

OAB-First Floor Program
HISTORIC OLD ADMINISTRATION BUILDING

Built in 1916, the Historic Old Administrative Building was the first permanent structure of Fresno State Normal School, now known as Fresno City College. The two-story, unreinforced masonry building has been unused since 1975 due to non-conformance with state seismic standards. Now, the 110,000-square-foot renovation, designed by ELS Architecture and Urban Design, will give the college 26 classrooms, large group instruction spaces, and administrative offices accommodating 2,000 students, as well as a 700-seat performing arts auditorium. The design team is rendering the seismic upgrade invisible to maintain the National Landmark's historic integrity by strengthening existing brick bearing walls with shotcrete walls layered on the interior sides of existing walls. To meet the State Center Community College District's academic needs in Fresno, the new program makes maximum use of existing classrooms, lecture rooms, offices and corridors, minimizing the use of materials and energy while preserving much of the architecture's original character. When the building reopens in early 2010, its many concerts, lectures, art exhibits, and educational and cultural activities will welcome both students and the community, which has been a driving force in maintaining this California educational icon.

83

ELS Architecture and Urban Design

Grand Theater Center for the Arts
Tracy, California

Tracy was founded in 1878 to serve the railroads in California's Central Valley and later the growing agricultural industry, but progress has bypassed its downtown for the last 30 years. Determined to revitalize its neglected downtown and fulfill the community's desire for a local arts education and performing arts facility, the city retained ELS Architecture and Urban Design to convert and link several historic buildings into the new Grand Theatre Center for the Arts. The two-level, 37,000-square-foot downtown arts center is now home to city-sponsored visual arts, ceramics and music classes, a 560-seat performing arts theater, a 120-seat black box theater, a dance studio and an art gallery. The restoration included the Grand Theatre – the city's landmark which opened in 1923 and added an Art Deco tower and marquee in 1939 – as well as a firehouse, town hall, and two hotel structures, all dating from the turn of the 20th century. The exterior of each historic building has been restored, and spaces between the exterior walls have been transformed into a new sky-lit circulation and lobby space. Breathing new life into the city's historic facades, the design celebrates the rich building variety and character of Tracy's historic downtown.

Left, top to bottom: Theater, art gallery, lobby and dance studio

Below: Exterior showing historic facades

Photography: David Wakely, Jennifer Reiley (theater)

Gould Evans

Gould Evans

South Junior High School
Lawrence, Kansas

Lawrence, Kansas strives to be a desirable community. This city of 85,000 residents is regularly cited as a college town "to which people most want to move" (*Reader's Digest*), one of "50 Best Small Metro Areas" to launch a business (*Inc.*) and one of the metropolitan areas with under 500,000 populations and "Best Metrowide" public schools

(*Expansion Management*). That's why Lawrence School District recently replaced its obsolete South Junior High School with a new, three-floor, 133,000-square-foot building designed by Gould Evans. The award-winning design includes classrooms, library, auditorium, visual arts, music, two gymnasiums, cafeteria, commons, administrative offices and

maintenance/ storage. Generously illuminated by skylights and windows, it incorporates facilities that are adaptable, accessible and conducive to group activity, including versatile two-story classroom and learning atrium spaces. The classrooms flank interstitial spaces or "pods" that provide additional space for group study, and selectively

share movable walls that let classes collaborate on group projects, share resources and increase workspaces as required. On a broader scale, the facility locates public and administrative spaces at the entry and other strategic positions in the academic wings to improve wayfinding, connectivity, safety and security during school and after hours. In short, it

reflects its much-admired community.

Above, left, center, right: Exterior, main entrance and outdoor seating area

Below left: Glass fronts of classrooms in corridor

Below right: Window in corridor overlooking grounds

Opposite: Corridor for one of two academic wings

Photography: Michael Spillers; Gould Evans Tristan Telander (below right)

JUNIOR HIGH

Gould Evans

Johnson County Community College
Regnier Center for Business and Technology
Overland Park, Kansas

Community colleges give 46 percent of U.S. undergraduates the job training, college preparation and continuing education they need, a responsibility Johnson County Community College, in Overland Park, Kansas, has conscientiously fulfilled since 1969. Consider the school's new, three-floor, 130,000-square-foot Regnier Center for Business and Technology, designed by Gould Evans. To serve curriculum courses, it offers laboratories for specific applications along with faculty offices and a 24/7 open laboratory. For the division of continuing education, it provides conference, seminar and breakout rooms, laboratories for specific applications, 300-seat con-

ference center with serving kitchen, and administrative offices. The information technology department also has space for offices, technology staging and setup work, conference rooms and campus-wide data center. Yet the award-winning building is also an outstanding learning environment where informal education extends beyond the classroom in a range of settings, including two that would shine anywhere. The atrium shared with the adjacent Nerman Museum of Contemporary Art, for example, is a stunning event venue that acts as a beacon on the school's 234-acre campus. As for the demonstration laboratory over the south entrance, it is

a showcase for social gatherings, special events and exhibits with partner businesses that raises the profile of community colleges.

Top left: Atrium shared with Nerman Museum of Contemporary Art

Top right, upper and lower: Longitudinal view of exterior and interior of demonstration laboratory

Above left: Staircase

Left: Exterior of demonstration laboratory

Opposite: South entrance with demonstration lab above

Photography: Michael Spillers, Timothy Hursley

Gould Evans

University of South Florida
Marshall Student Center
Tampa, Florida

Left: Main entrance with copper-clad canopy

Above: Entrance with copper-clad volume

Below left: Main corridor on north-south a xis

Bottom left: Retail store

Opposite: Atrium

Photography: Al Hurley

Since the University of South Florida was founded in 1956 as the first public university to serve Florida's emerging urban regions, starting with five buildings and 2,000 students in Tampa, it has become an increasingly influential institution, enrolling 46,000 students on campuses in Tampa, St. Petersburg, Sarasota-Manatee and Lakeland. Like many other colleges and universities, it recently gave its Tampa student center a more meaningful role to play in shaping the campus experience. In fact, the new four-story, 233,000-square-foot Marshall Student Center, designed by Gould Evans, introduces a campus "living room" that is firmly integrated with campus life and campus pathways, offering extensive dining options, retail stores, ballroom, auditorium, Senate Chamber, meeting/conference rooms, offices for student activities and administration, computer laboratory and outdoor programming spaces. The key to the design's effectiveness is a scheme that groups program elements in pavilions that can be visually and physically reached from its four-story atrium, the heart of the "living room" that internalizes the campus's main north-south axis using full-height curtain wall systems and cable-rail systems along the atrium's walkways. Outside, the axis is highlighted with two copper-clad elliptical forms destined to become campus icons for students and alumni alike.

Gould Evans

University of Arizona
Law Commons at James E. Rogers College of Law
Tucson, Arizona

Because the James E. Rogers College of Law at the University of Arizona, in Tucson, has been small by choice since its beginning in 1915, enrolling some 150 students in each entering class and a total student body of about 500, educators were concerned that the law library lacked visual presence, functioning as a student gathering place only by convenience. Now, following a three-level, 113,694-square-foot renovation, designed by Gould Evans, students appear at every opportunity. To transform the space, the design team created a "destination" library that celebrates the law. The remodeling, involving the library, classrooms, lounges, student publication office, student organization office, computer laboratories and faculty and administrative offices, deliberately blurs the boundaries where library spaces meet student spaces, common areas, information desk and circulation desk. Increasing open space and installing soft seating areas and open-study tables spaces required compact shelving to store the library's collection. However, the impact of openness, visibility, daylight and enhanced communication at the law commons has been unmistakable. Toni M. Massaro, dean of the college, concludes, "You have given our students a place that tells them who they are—who they might become at their best—and they get it."

Right: New exterior with sunscreen

Lower right: Stair to library's lower level

Below right: Remodeled stairwell

Lower left: Lobby

Bottom left: Open-study tables and seating

Photography: Roland Bishop, Caleb Alvarado

GUND Partnership

GUND Partnership

University of Massachusetts Amherst
Studio Arts Building
Amherst, Massachusetts

At a prime point of entry at University of Massachusetts Amherst, the 51,000-square-foot Studio Arts Building, designed by GUND Partnership, creates a new campus gateway and promotes community among the various arts programs that were previously scattered around the school's 1450-acre campus. Fostering a multidisciplinary approach to art, the building combines specialized instructional studios and workshops, studios for undergraduates, graduate students, and faculty, pin-up and critique areas, exhibit spaces, and communal gathering spaces. Its V-shaped plan is anchored by the transparent Commons Cube, which creates an axial focal point within the eastern campus district, and also serves as the main entrance and gathering place for art students. This central commons is just one of the many design features that encourage interaction and support the social component of the creative process. Informal pin-up and critique areas are woven into the fabric of the circulation spine, and transparent and translucent windows reveal activities within the studios. The design heralds a new generation of arts facilities by increasing collegiality among arts students and inspiring safer practices and "greener" art techniques, while also showcasing the importance of arts on this major public research university.

Top: Exterior, courtyard and amphitheater

Above left: Commons Cube at night

Left: Undergraduate studios

Below: Main stair

Opposite: View from Commons Cube's upper level

Photography: Robert Benson

GUND Partnership

Kenyon College
Peirce Hall
Gambier, Ohio

The recently finished 69,000-square-foot renovation and expansion of Kenyon's Peirce Hall, designed by GUND Partnership, reestablishes the historic c. 1929 Gothic Revival dining hall as a social center on campus, while updating food service operations and supporting the College's larger sustainable mission. With a striking blend of old and new, the addition follows the form of the historic hall and is linked by a new glass atrium connector. This dynamic space establishes a new circulation spine for the entire complex, and leads to the new 12-station marketplace servery, a showcase for food preparation. New design features and "green" technologies, such as an expanded loading dock, flash freezers, and a pulper extractor that converts food waste into compost material, support the delivery of food from local farmers and enabled the expansion of the College's existing Farm to Table local food program. The historic Great Hall was restored to its original glory, while new dining spaces reinterpret its grandeur with contemporary details. The new Thomas Hall features expansive windows, with panoramic views to the surrounding campus. Five lower level dining rooms for public dining and private events, an expanded pub, along with administrative and student organization offices make Peirce a vibrant center for 21st century campus life.

Above: The atrium link to the servery

Left and far left: Thomas Hall

Opposite clockwise: Great Hall, pub, servery

Photography: David Lamb

97

GUND Partnership

Kenyon College Athletic Center
Gambier, Ohio

Merging athletic, recreational, academic, and social functions, Kenyon College's new, three-floor, 250,000-square-foot Athletic Center, designed by GUND Partnership, creates a new hub for campus life. The Center reflects educators' current thinking that fitness and recreational facilities can form the core of communal meeting places. Equipped with a 50-meter swimming pool, tennis courts, squash courts, weight room, fieldhouse/running track, and training rooms, along with a theater and film library, multi-purpose rooms, study lounges, café, and offices, it allows students sharing a wide range of interests to come together not only for individual fitness and recreation, but also in teams, in groups, and as an entire campus. The design itself offers a fresh counterpoint to Kenyon's Collegiate Gothic campus. Its barn or shed-like form—essentially an aluminum and glass curtainwall enclosing an exposed steel structure—was inspired by traditional rural vernacular and occupies a grassy flood plain below the primary ridge of the historic campus. Sustainable design features, including low-e glass, low albedo membrane roof, enhanced insulation, internally louvered glass, and automatic roller shades for daylight control, contribute to significant energy savings. Students enter its transparent core and head to different venues via well-defined corridors and a grand stair. Carefully planned open vistas allow students to participate in the full array of sports, fitness, and social activities, shaping Kenyon's spirit of community.

Top left: Grand staircase

Top right: Exterior from playing fields

Above right: 50-meter swimming pool

Right: Fieldhouse and running track

Opposite bottom: Intramural court

Photography: David Lamb

GUND Partnership

The Ohio State University
William Oxley Thompson Library
Columbus, Ohio

Above right: West reading room

Right: Southwest view of exterior

Below left: North-south cross section

Bottom left: West atrium

Illustration: Courtesy of GUND Partnership

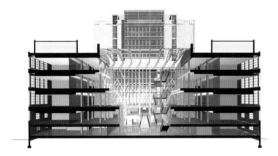

The William Oxley Thompson Library is the main library of The Ohio State University, in Columbus. The original Beaux Arts structure was built in 1913, and underwent renovations in 1951 and 1977. Located at the heart of the campus, at the western terminus of the historic Oval, the library remains a symbolic and intellectual crossroads. However, to acknowledge recent changes in campus life, library design, technology applications, and service delivery, it is now undergoing a thorough,

100,000-square-foot expansion and 220,000-square-foot renovation, designed by GUND Partnership as design architect with George Acock Associates as architect of record. The design team's strategy focuses on establishing a more coherent, symmetrical organization by introducing two atria, new entrances, and a more efficient pattern for internal pedestrian movement. This includes the design of the new west addition. Its focus is a new reading room on the west side, which "mirrors" the historic

1913 reading room on the east. The fulcrum of the building is the 1951 tower, updated and retained as the repository of the 1.2 million print collection. To the east and west of the tower are the two sky-lit atria, which introduce natural light and a sense of spaciousness into the library core. In addition to restoring Thompson Library's original grandeur, the project will keep Ohio State on the forefront of education as it marks its 140th year in 2010.

Hammond Beeby Rupert Ainge Inc.

Hammond Beeby Rupert Ainge, Inc.

Southern Methodist University
Meadows Museum
Dallas, Texas

What do Velázquez, Ribera, Zurbarán, El Greco, Murillo, Goya, Miró and Picasso share with Dallas, Texas? The answer, as art scholars and residents of "Big D" know, is the Meadows Museum of Southern Methodist University, housing one of the largest and finest collections of Spanish art outside Spain. SMU has showcased the masterpieces acquired by Texas philanthropist and oil financier Algur H. Meadows since 1965. However, because the collection has continued to grow during its four decades at SMU, it is too large for the original, 11,000-square-foot Meadows Museum that Meadows helped to construct as part of SMU's emerging arts center. The new, two-story, 65,000-square-foot Meadows Museum, designed by Hammond Beeby Rupert Ainge, dramatically expands the institution's horizons with state-of-the-art facilities for its permanent collection, traveling exhibits, print study and storage, art storage, exhibit preparation, auditorium, classrooms, offices, reception room, restaurant and museum store. In addition, the design economically accommodates a 600-car parking facility on site by locating the parking underground and placing the building above it on a raised courtyard. The building sits on this plinth to effectively mediate between the adjacent dormitories to the north and the football stadium to the east. Honoring the same Palladian tradition that inspires the Collegiate Georgian buildings on campus, the Meadows Museum immediately identifies itself as a cultural landmark.

Hammond Beeby Rupert Ainge, Inc.

Millennium Park
Exelon Pavilions
Chicago, Illinois

The power of public space is demonstrated daily at Chicago's Millennium Park, a 24.5-acre oasis developed by the city and philanthropic community with world-renowned architects, planners, artists and designers. The public loves the award-winning environment much as the critics do for making urban space accessible, enjoyable and even inspirational. Besides such highlights as the Pritzker Pavilion, an outdoor concert venue designed by Frank Gehry, the contemporary Lurie Garden, designed by Gustafson Guthrie Nichol Ltd., Piet Oudolf and Robert Israel, and Anish Kapoor's popular Cloud Gate sculpture. Two of the four Exelon Pavilions located at the north end convert solar energy into electricity, helping Chicago to become America's "Green Capital." The LEED Silver-certified northeast and northwest Pavilions, designed by Hammond Beeby Rupert Ainge, are two- and three-story, 11,500-square-foot minimalist black cubes that generate power and complement the neighboring Harris Theater for Music and Dance, also designed by Hammond Beeby Rupert Ainge.

Inside, visitors find exhibition/display/information zones, offices, a gift shop and transportation access for Chicago Park District personnel and the Exelon Corporation. Architecturally the skin is a double-walled system

consisting of an outer photovoltaic curtain wall separated by an air cavity from an inner fire-rated thermal wall generates electricity, keeping the promise of renewable energy bright in Chicago.

Top: Exterior

Above: Photovoltaic display mirrored in reflective ceiling panels

Left: Pavilion seen against Chicago skyline

Below left: Harris Theater and Exelon Pavilions

Opposite: View from interior

Photography: Hedrich Blessing

Hammond Beeby Rupert Ainge, Inc.

Yale University
Sterling Memorial Library, Bass Library Renovation and Addition
New Haven, Connecticut

Over time, even the most forward-looking colleges and universities need updating. Consider the new Anne T. and Robert M. Bass Library at Yale University's venerable Sterling Memorial Library in New Haven, Connecticut. The two-level, 72,383-square-foot renovation and new construction, designed by Hammond Beeby Rupert Ainge, totally transforms the Cross Campus Library, Sterling's 1971 underground addition. Not only has increased use of digital media required technological upgrades, such evolving study patterns as group study and online collaboration called for flexible, innovative spaces. In addition, elevated user expectations made improvements in service amenities almost as essential as repairs and upgrades to the buildings' envelope, mechanical systems and finishes. The transformation is dramatic. While Bass still houses Cross Campus's 150,000-volume core collection, it invigorates the learning environment with open study areas, electronic classrooms, outdoor reading courtyards, group study rooms, lounge and café, accommodating today's study habits. To strengthen the link to Sterling, a new, daylighted communicating stair leads to a new lower-level reading room, restrooms and staff offices, as well as a redesigned connecting tunnel to Bass. The new interiors are equally compelling, sweeping away a nondescript modern setting to establish a Collegiate Gothic milieu worthy of Yale's three-century-old campus.

Above: New entry pavilion

Above right: Stair from connecting tunnel to Bass

Below right: Reading tables in collections area

Opposite bottom, left to right: Group study room, view of outdoor reading courtyard, café/study lounge

Photography: Tim Hursley

Hammond Beeby Rupert Ainge, Inc.

Clio Hall, Renovation and Addition
Princeton University
Princeton, New Jersey

Clio Hall is one of two identical marble Ionic-style Greek Revival temples on the Princeton campus. Designed by A. Page Brown in 1892, Clio Hall and its counterpart Whig Hall were erected for the two debating societies on campus at the time. Clio Hall is now the central location for the Graduate School offices, thanks to a renovation and addition designed by Hammond Beeby Rupert Ainge. The makeover, including some office space for Undergraduate Admission as well as new ADA and code-compliant circulation, respects the building's history and position on the south end of the historic campus core. Since the renovation program called for a complete systems replacement, new exit stair and elevator, the vertical services occupy an addition at the south side of the structure with a new accessible entrance. The addition mirrors in plan the projecting front portico and matches the original Vermont marble cladding in detail, depth and finish. Consequently, Clio Hall enters its second century equipped, including new mechanical and electrical systems and modern offices that complement its 19th-century architecture, and an addition that maintains the historic character of the exterior.

Top: Addition

Upper left: Refurbished stair hall

Upper right: Clio Hall, foreground, and Whig Hall, background

Above left: Reception/lobby

Left: Elevation with portico

Photography: Barry Halkin

Hastings & Chivetta

Hastings & Chivetta

Lindenwood University
J. Scheidegger Center for the Arts
St. Charles, Missouri

One of the joys of a college town is the cultural life residents share with the local college or university. The citizens of St. Charles, Missouri, site of Lindenwood University, are certainly as pleased as the students about the new, three-level, 135,000-square-foot J. Scheidegger Center for the Arts, designed by Hastings & Chivetta. In addition to consolidating the departments of instrumental and vocal music, and costume and fashion design, at one location on Lindenwood's 500-acre campus, the Center brings major performing artists to town. The building provides its constituents such principal facilities as the 1,200-seat theater with balcony, black box theater, TV studio and art gallery on the main and upper levels, and the orchestra pit, trap, mechanical rooms and storage on the lower level, along with classrooms, music studios, rehearsal halls, office suites, event kitchen and lounges. Since the Fine & Performing Arts Division teaches students both the practical and theoretical aspects of their areas of study, the building comes professionally equipped for theater and television studio operations. As for the architecture, it skillfully captures the scale, proportions and materials of the campus vernacular, blending with structures from the 1800s as well as those as new as itself.

Above: Lobby of the Four Squares

Left: Band room

Far left: 1,200-seat theater with balcony

Below left: Dressing room

Below far left TV studio

Opposite: Exterior

Photography: Sam Fentress Photography and Lindenwood University

Hastings & Chivetta

Centre College
Crounse Academic Center
Danville, Kentucky

You can't turn back the clock, but the new Crounse Academic Center at Centre College, in Danville, Kentucky, shows how effectively good design can integrate past, present and future. The four-level, 100,000-square-foot structure, designed by Hastings & Chivetta, renovates and expands the existing 70,678-square-foot Doherty Library as part of a larger scheme that introduces new classrooms, faculty offices and other facilities. Of course, the heart of the new building is the Doherty Library. Here, construction has produced not only high-density stacks for 60,000 more volumes, but also state-of-the-art reading and study rooms, a meeting room, 4,700 square feet for circulation, reference and archives, and a new Center for Teaching and Learning, which comprises a 170-seat movie theater, high-technology classrooms, projectors, A/V equipment and smartboards. Connected to the library by way of a spacious shared lobby and grand staircase are the new faculty/staff offices, lounges, seminar/meeting rooms, lecture hall, media center and computer laboratories that give the Crounse Academic Center its larger mission. But in a neat twist of architectural history, the library's undistinguished 1960s-modernist façade has been transformed into a Federal-style edifice of brick and limestone that evokes the first campus building, circa 1819, that once occupied the site.

Above: Remodeled façade
Above right: Catalogue room
Opposite bottom, left to right: 170-seat movie theatre, lobby, seminar/meeting room
Photography: Sam Fentress Photography

Hastings & Chivetta

Hanover College
Hendricks Hall Renovation
Hanover, Indiana

Buildings like Hendricks Hall, built in 1903 and now revered as a landmark by Hanover College, in Hanover, Indiana, have more than one life. The second oldest building on Hanover's 650-acre campus, the 6,760-square-foot, brick-and-limestone Beaux Arts structure is a tribute to Thomas Hendricks, alumnus, governor of Indiana and vice president of the United States, financed by his widow, Eliza Hendricks. After serving as the college's first library, it has sheltered elementary education, fine arts, foreign languages and computers. In its latest transformation, designed

by Hastings & Chivetta, Hendricks Hall has become the home of the Rivers Institute, a multi-disciplinary academic program that conducts cultural, economic and scientific studies of rivers. The successful renovation of the facility, besides providing up-to-date office suites, library, and meeting rooms, has raised its building systems to contemporary standards for safety, security and accessibility without compromising its historic integrity. Thus, visitors are delighted to see the central dome restored to its radiant glory, the reading and study room preserving the former librarian's office,

displaying the refurbished original shelves and cabinets along with a panoramic view of the Ohio River, and a high-technology video conferencing room, connecting century-old Hendricks Hall with international organizations worldwide.

Above: Exterior

Top right: Conference room

Above right: Reading and study room

Right: Private office

Opposite: Central dome in lobby

Photography: Sam Fentress Photography

Hastings & Chivetta

University of Tulsa
Collins Hall
Tulsa, Oklahoma

When the University of Tulsa, a private university founded in 1894, commissioned Hastings & Chivetta to update its 1995 Master Plan and to prepare a campus-wide Space Utilization Study, the architects identified projects that seemed critical to the wellbeing of the campus. One of several projects Hastings & Chivetta was subsequently invited to design has given the university a new gateway that is as impressive as it is functional. Collins Hall is a two-story, 39,103-square-foot welcome center and administrative facility whose Collegiate Gothic-style architecture in ashlar stone, stone trim and slate tile is anchored by a monumental three-story entry tower. Located at the end of a new, three-block-long campus green running perpendicular to a major thoroughfare at the edge of the university, the award-winning building houses a number of key functions. Along with the president's administrative suite, alumni offices, development offices, such student-focused functions as admissions and financial aid (now conveniently assembled in one location), and Heritage Room (displaying historic memorabilia), there is the 2,000-square-foot lobby that serves as the university's "living room," whose gracious and comfortable space has the flexibility to host special events—a 21st-century gateway for the University of Tulsa.

Top: Entry tower

Above: Front elevation

Right, in descending order: President's office, lobby

Photography: Reyndell Photography

HMC Architects

3546 Concours Street • Ontario, CA 91764 • 909.989.9979 • (F) 909.483.1400

www.hmcarchitects.com

HMC Architects

Alvord Unified School District
Innovative Learning Center
Riverside, California

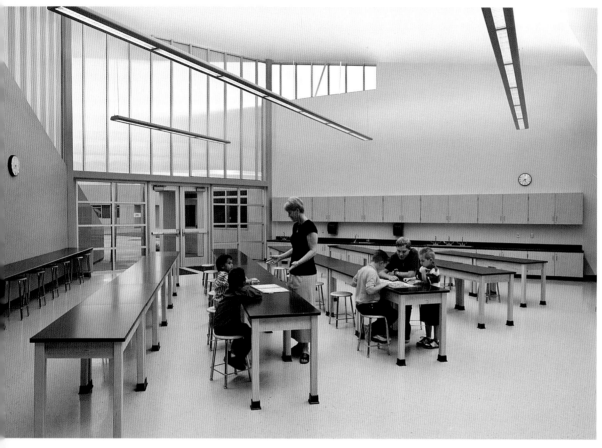

Left: Flexible laboratory space

Below left: Typical exterior

Bottom left: Library

Opposite: Building and circulation path

Photography: Claudia Ambriz, HMC Architects, and Tom Bonner

To accommodate a unique pre-K–6 curriculum and host college-level teacher training and accreditation programs, Alvord Unified School District, in Riverside, California, has joined forces with Riverside Community College, La Sierra University, and Riverside County Department of Health to develop the Innovative Learning Center. The new, one-story, 103,000-square-foot project for 1,200 students (720 K-6, 180 preschool and 300 college), designed by HMC Architects, places nine freestanding structures on a campus adjacent to La Sierra University. The award-winning design interweaves buildings, courtyards, and walkways to provide learning opportunities at every turn. Besides such accommodations as classrooms, library, kitchen/cafeteria, administration offices, teacher observation areas, wellness center, and multi-purpose facilities for neighborhood events, there are outdoor breakout spaces and flexible teaching areas as well as learning elements integrated in walls, walkway patterns and seating areas. The care taken to fulfill educators' goals is clearly visible inside the main facility. Each of the six "villages" at the on-site Phillip M. Stokoe Elementary School features learning suites that house many learning areas in a single space. Planned for traditional, grade-based programs or multi-level student groups organized around a single theme or activity, the studios support personalized education within the larger school, an elusive goal for conventional educational environments.

HMC Architects

Los Angeles Unified School District
High School for the Visual and Performing Arts
Los Angeles, California

Right: Grand stairway

Far right: Crystalline lobby and tower of theater school

Above right: Aerial view of campus

Opposite above left: Library cone and view through campus

Opposite above right: Sculptural tower, under construction

Illustration: Chris Grant, HMC Architects

Photography: Claudia Ambriz, HMC Architects

A remarkable academic community is rising at a promontory in downtown Los Angeles. The High School for the Visual and Performing Arts, by HMC Architects as executive architect and Coop Himmelb(l)au of Austria as designer of record, will exemplify the Los Angeles Unified School District's academic model for a small learning community. Some 450 students in each of four academic communities will pursue general and arts-specific studies, occupying a section of a 9.8-acre campus with appropriate facilities for dance, theater, music and visual arts education. The design features seven contemporary buildings in concrete, metal and glass enclosing 238,000 square feet of space. These highly futuristic forms encircling the cone-shaped library provide classrooms, library, administration, gymnasium, dance rehearsal and studio spaces, music studios, visual arts studios, 1,000-seat performance theater with lobby, black box theater, fly loft and scene shop, student quadrangle, athletic field and gathering spaces. They will also act as transitional elements to coordinate the site's 40-foot grade differential, establishing a plaza level defined by architecture on the periphery and protected interior space at the center. With the Disney Concert Hall, Museum of Contemporary Art and Cathedral of Our Lady of Angels as neighbors, the complex will be a flagship school of the LAUSD.

HMC Architects

University of California, San Diego
Rady School of Management
La Jolla, California

Located at the northwest corner of the University of California, San Diego's campus in La Jolla, the Rady School of Management's design is a thoughtful response to both academic and corporate communities, expressed through this dynamic, four-story, 90,000-square-foot facility.

The completed building is Phase I of a planned two-phased building campus (totaling approximately 170,000 square feet). Phase II is scheduled for completion in 2011. HMC Architects (design architect) partnered with Ellerbe Becket (prime architect), led the design of this unique

education environment, which expresses the vision of the new school; one of innovative and revolutionary exploration in business and management. The facility houses an array of instructional, student, faculty, and administrative functions including career services, executive education, tiered

classrooms and multipurpose spaces. Phase II will add more of these functions, along with an auditorium and a research center. The design celebrates its location in a palette of textures and colors found in the campus fabric and the open design allows for impressive views of the nearby ocean and surrounding San Diego mountains. Robert Sullivan, dean of the Rady School of Management, recently observed, "The success of this project was in how the design captured our spirit through careful listening and collaboration."

Above: Phase II rendering

Far left: River walk entrance

Left: Tiered classroom

Below left: Upper terrance and bridges

Below and bottom right: Corner balconies

Photography: David Rova and David Fennema, HMC Architects

Illustration: Chris Grant, HMC Architects

HMC Architects

Los Angeles County
High School for the Arts
Los Angeles, California

The 570 students of Los Angeles County High School for the Arts or "Arts High," one of the premier public arts high schools in the western United States, will soon occupy a versatile new facility on the campus of California State University, Los Angeles. This three-level, 42,000-square-foot building, designed by HMC Architects, takes a layered, multi-functional approach to planning, so its spaces will double as "messy" production areas and elegant exhibit halls. As a pragmatic, hands-on environment, it stacks classrooms at ground level, larger art studios on the second tier, and a black box theater on top; gives academic spaces similar sizes for efficiency and economy; and divides the site into the more formal entry area and informal "work yard." Few interior walls are load bearing, since the building employs a specialized moment frame structure, granting considerable latitude for adjustments. (Sharing the Cal State campus, it complies with a mandatory LEED Silver rating for sustainability.) But the school also knows how to put on a show. Reflective glazing and dramatic lighting will transform the black box theater at nightfall, as a large event board on its public side tells the audience, "It's showtime!"

HOLT Architects, P.C.

HOLT Architects, P.C.

State University of New York
Upstate Medical University, Setnor Academic Building
Syracuse, New York

The first new classroom space built on the State University of New York Upstate Medical University's Syracuse campus in nearly three decades occupies an understated brick and limestone structure that reveals its modern identity inside a dazzling, four-story atrium. The five-story, 48,000-square-foot Setnor Academic Building, designed by HOLT Architects, provides generic academic space and a state-of-the-art clinical skills center to an institution founded as Geneva Medical College in 1834. Its atrium plays a pivotal role by connecting classrooms, offices, alumni association suite and clinical skills center to historic Weiskotten Hall on three levels and maintaining a crossroads for scholarly interaction and public events. To preserve Weiskotten Hall's existing windows, the new structure employs its neighbor's north wall as well as its own south wall to frame the atrium between them, placing a 100-foot-long skylight overhead to flood the space with daylight. However, while the architecture defers to the older facility in form, scale and materials (while simultaneously observing sustainable design principles), the interior makes no such compromises for healthcare. Among the Clinical Skills Teaching Center's 22 examination rooms, closed-circuit monitoring and advanced medical equipment, tomorrow's doctors are perfecting their "bedside manner" and clinical skills for a 21st-century world.

Below left: Classroom
Below right: Entry
Bottom left: Conference room
Opposite: Atrium
Photography: Tom Watson, Robert Mescavage (atrium)

HOLT Architects, P.C.

Wells College
Ann Wilder Stratton '46 Hall
Aurora, New York

Creating academic workplaces where scientists can communicate with students and colleagues as well as conduct research is yielding impressive results on the nation's campuses. At Wells College, an esteemed liberal arts college in Aurora, New York founded in 1868, the new Ann Wilder Stratton '46 Hall, designed by HOLT Architects, represents an intriguing example. The three-story, 46,000-square-foot structure provides flexible arrangements for science classrooms and turns faculty members' offices, teaching laboratories and research laboratories into effective units for interaction and research. Yet it also serves the entire campus. Its 91-seat lecture hall is a showpiece combining a sloped floor, intimate scale and modern A/V technologies to accommodate daily academic use as well as guest lecturers. In addition,

its light-infused, two-story atrium, the hinge linking the L-shaped facility's two wings, hosts receptions and informal gatherings, while its corridors widen at points for gathering and are dotted with display cases, tack boards, benches and whiteboards to promote casual encounters. The building records a milestone for its predecessor as well. While Stratton Hall brings a sensitive contemporary design to a campus of historic brick-clad architecture, the 1906 facility it replaces, too costly to update for science, has started a new academic life.

Top: Lecture hall
Above: Exterior
Right: Atrium arcade
Below right: Laboratory
Opposite: Atrium with niches displaying fossil collection
Photography: Tom Watson

HOLT Architects, P.C.

Cazenovia College
Art & Design Building
Cazenovia, New York

Ever since Cazenovia College was founded in 1824 as a Methodist seminary in Cazenovia, New York, the respected, non-denominational college has participated in community life. So when the school announced a new home for its art and design department on a site one block from the village's Albany Street Historic District, it wanted a landmark that residents would welcome. The award-winning two-story, 24,000-square-foot Art & Design Building, designed by HOLT Architects, greets visitors to the campus with a structure that reflects village history while providing a modern facility that is larger than it appears. Though the design's brick, limestone and copper exterior is tied to campus architecture, its mass is divided into four linked "houses," complete with steeply pitched roofs and gable ends, that are similar in scale to nearby homes. Inside, a central circulation spine anchored by a two-story atrium connects state-of-the-art classrooms, graphic arts studios, interior design studios, photography darkroom suite and faculty offices, as well as a gallery in the corner closest to the village, where the public can view the work of students, faculty and invited artists. Says Scotty Ottaviano, Cazenovia professor of interior design, "We are very fortunate to have such a beautiful location."

Top right: Computer classroom
Upper right: Gallery
Right: Exterior
Opposite: Atrium
Photography: Tom Watson

HOLT Architects, P.C.

Colgate University
Glendening Boathouse
Hamilton, New York

Left: Exterior on lakeside

Below left: Crew bay

Below right: Multi-purpose room

Photography: Tom Watson

Immediately after the ribbon-cutting ceremony and reception, Colgate University's new two-story, 11,400-square-foot Glendening Boathouse was put to good use, as Colgate's men's and women's crews competed against Hamilton, St. Lawrence and Bucknell, posting wins in every varsity race. Of course, the magnificent timber structure, designed by HOLT Architects, is as much a part of collegiate tradition as the crews. Its distinctive form, clad in red cedar shingles atop a bluestone base, has antecedents in the great 19th-century boathouses of the Schuylkill and Charles Rivers. Located on Lake Moraine, close to Colgate's campus in Hamilton, New York, the design serves both intercollegiate and recreational boating programs while fitting seamlessly into a community of lakeside homes. It's a spacious volume comprising four equal, 24-foot by 75-foot rectangular bays (two crew bays, one recreational bay, and one bay for offices and locker rooms) along with a large, multipurpose room for meetings and training on the second floor, where balconies overlook the lake. But because the mass is visually reduced by the low eave lines of the hip roofs, which contain much of the actual building volume, the boathouse honors the form, scale and spirit of the neighborhood. After all, that, too, is traditional.

Kallmann McKinnell & Wood Architects, Inc.

Kallmann McKinnell & Wood Architects, Inc.

Wesleyan University
Suzanne Lemberg Usdan University Center
Middletown, Connecticut

Small, prestigious and enlightened by a tradition begun in 1831 as a Methodist institution (school and church separated in 1937), Wesleyan University, in Middletown, Connecticut, has discovered the value of a student union even with just 2,700 full-time undergraduates and 200 graduate students on its 360-acre campus. The new, three-floor, 87,000-square-foot Usdan University Center, designed by Kallmann McKinnell & Wood Architects, establishes a gathering place students, staff, faculty, alumni and visitors can share. Its comprehensive accommodations include student dining, post office, café, student organizations, administration, ballroom, and spaces for music, dance and theater, along with lounges, terraces and courtyard. While the site, adjacent to the Fayerweather Building and historic College Row, positioned the brick, slate and brownstone-clad contemporary structure in a central location, it also posed significant challenges. Not only did the low elevation and transitional-style façade help integrate the Center with its neighbors, the structural design accommodates utility lines running beneath it and inserts an all-new steel structure inboard of Fayerweather's masonry exterior. Of course, none of this inconveniences anyone at the Center, where a centralized plan, sunny, spacious interiors, and modern furnishings based on a white oak and white terrazzo color scheme make it the "in" place.

Kallmann McKinnell & Wood Architects, Inc.

Reading Area Community College
Miller Center for the Arts
Reading, Pennsylvania

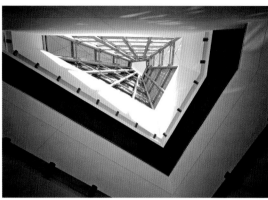

You can't miss Reading Area Community College's handsome new Miller Center for the Arts, designed by Kallmann McKinnell & Wood Architects, when you approach downtown Reading, Pennsylvania. The strikingly modern, two-level, 23,500-square-foot structure, clad in brick, aluminum and glass and topped by a sloping zinc roof and trapezoidal glass skylight, stands at the Penn Street Bridge and Second Street, one of Reading's busiest intersections and major entry points. If the Center seems equally accessible to theatergoers and scholars, it should. The College, founded by the Reading School District in 1971 and now sponsored by Berks County, has always blurred the distinction between "town" and "gown" by providing associate degrees and other educational programs to enhance the economic vitality of the region. Accordingly, the Center's double-height lobby faces the street behind a transparent curtain wall, drawing public attention to a facility that includes a 500-seat endstage/proscenium theater with balcony, 2,400-square-foot stage with modified fly loft, scene shop and storage, dressing and green rooms, concession, coat room and box office. In effect, it's two facilities in one: a superb venue for academic courses, student-organized events, and faculty/staff seminars, and a versatile performing arts center inviting outstanding artists to Reading.

Top: Exterior
Above: Skylight
Above left: Evening view showing lobby
Left: Proscenium theater
Opposite: Lobby
Photography: Gordon Schenck

Kallmann McKinnell & Wood Architects, Inc.

Case Western Reserve University
Mandel Center for Nonprofit Organizations
Cleveland, Ohio

When Case Western Reserve University chose to develop its new, two-story, 25,000-square-foot Mandel Center for Nonprofit Organizations on the site of a former community garden in a residential neighborhood of Cleveland, it worked diligently with Kallmann McKinnell & Wood Architects to create a building and landscape with a distinctive sense of place. Their effort has been abundantly rewarded. Although the structure houses a range of facilities, including first-floor spaces shared by Case Western with the community, such as technology-enhanced classrooms designed for easy reconfiguration, meeting spaces, a student lounge with fireplace, and a courtyard surrounded by a Honduran mahogany pergola, as well as offices on the second floor, it fits comfortably among the neighborhood's two- and three-story houses. Such elements as the horizontal profile, abundant windows, front yard with welcoming porch and courtyard with pergola preserve the memory of the garden as well as the scale of the neighborhood. Inside the building's brick, glass and aluminum exterior, the modern interior is spacious, airy, flooded with daylight and views, and appointed in comfortable, cleanly detailed modern furnishings. Commending the contextual design of the Center, Steven Litt, architecture critic of the *Cleveland Plain Dealer*, recently noted, "It's magical."

Above: Offices

Right: Exterior on residential street

Below: Classroom

Opposite bottom: Courtyard and student lounge

Photography: Alan Karchmer

Kallmann McKinnell & Wood Architects in association with Wou & Partners (now HGA Architects & Engineers)

University of California, Riverside
Physical Sciences Building
Riverside, California

Established as the Citrus Experiment Station by the California State Legislature in 1907, the University of California, Riverside has developed into a world-class, research-oriented institution, likening its 1,200-acre campus to a "living laboratory" where 14,571 undergraduates and 2,051 graduate students work with state-of-the-art resources. One of the newest examples of its passion for research, the four-floor, 130,765-square-foot Physical Sciences Build-

ing, designed by Kallmann McKinnell & Wood Architects, shows how architecture can shape the campus as well as the curriculum. At the edge of a developing Sciences precinct, the structure employs a courtyard configuration to define a new campus space off the primary pedestrian circulation route and provide a focal point for future development. Though LEED certification was not requested, the school encouraged the design team to apply green design principles, resulting

in extensive use of exterior sun-shading devices that give lightness and texture to the façades. Space within the masonry walls is similarly exploited. While continuous tracks of laboratory space satisfy current needs and anticipate future changes, offices are stacked in four vertical suites at the center and served by skylit stairs, providing rich opportunities for informal encounters. At UC Riverside, good design gets a good workout.

Above left: View from Campus Drive

Above right: Courtyard and North-South Campus Walk, and typical laboratory

Photography: Tom Bonner

Perkins Eastman

Perkins Eastman

Chongqing Library
Chongqing, China

For Chongqing, a port city in the mountainous, forested upper reaches of the Yangtze River in southwest China with some 31 million residents and a 3,000-year history, the new, six-level, 540,000-square-foot Chongqing Library had to be much more than a collection of books. Often called "Mountain City" for its majestic natural topography, Chongqing wanted an educational, cultural, and social center where knowledge and ideas could be studied and shared. Accordingly, comprehensive planning and design, careful site development, and the use of traditional and local building materials have produced a stunning cultural and civic icon, designed by Perkins Eastman, featuring

an exhibition and lecture hall, gallery space, conference facilities, a guest suite for visiting scholars as well as multiple reading rooms, an auditorium, and café. The library honors the past and serves the future through a modern structure that evokes traditional Chinese architecture by grouping the three main programmatic elements, the open public access zone, secure public zone and private secure zone, around a center courtyard garden and reflecting pool. Harmonizing glass-sheathed interiors that benefit from transparency, stonewalled enclosures, and the courtyard garden, the library offers a unique resource to one of China's most dynamic commercial centers.

Top right and upper left and right: Exterior views

Directly above: Reading room

Right: Interior atrium detail

Opposite: Interior of Periodical Reading Room

Photography: Tim Griffith, ZhiHui Gu

Perkins Eastman

High Point University
Slane Student Center
High Point, North Carolina

Opened jointly by the Methodist Protestant Church (now the United Methodist Church) and the City of High Point, North Carolina, High Point University has progressed steadily from three partially completed buildings, nine faculty members and 122 students in 1924. Today, the school has a 145-acre campus, 40-plus buildings, 168 faculty members and 3,400 students—and is doubling its investment in academic programs, student life, scholarships and construction of new facilities. Perkins Eastman is providing extensive services for the campaign. From master planning, site selection for buildings, and traffic and parking studies to programming, architecture, construction services and project management for individual buildings, Perkins Eastman is developing facilities to enhance student-centered amenities and services needed by students to succeed in academia and beyond. The renovation of Slane Student Center, adding a two-story, 44,000-square-foot Student Activity Center for a total of 90,000 square feet, is surely its most visible project. While the exterior complements the university's Collegiate Georgian campus, students find the new and/or remodeled bookstore, dining services, multi-level fitness and athletic facilities, including a new pool and pool house, "express" locker rooms, stores for major retail chains, including Starbucks, Chick-Fil-A and Subway, and offices for student and career services are better than ever.

Below: Poolside facilities
Right: Fitness area
Opposite top left: Exterior
Opposite top right: Gym and running track
Photography: Tim Buchman

Perkins Eastman

Concordia International School
Shanghai, China

With global enterprises arriving in Shanghai, a leading business center in China with some 17 million residents, young families have flocked to the Concordia International School Shanghai since its founding in 1998. This pre-K to twelfth-grade, Lutheran-affiliated institution prepares 1,000 students for admission to U.S. schools, colleges and universities. Looking ahead, Concordia recently added two new freestanding structures to its campus, the 64,600-square-foot elementary school and 24,000-square-foot David F. Rittman Fine Arts Center, both designed by Perkins Eastman, which also prepared the school's master plan. The facilities are as progressive as Concordia itself. The new pre-K-4 elementary school is a self-contained environment that supports multiple ways of learning and fosters creativity by encouraging interaction between students and teachers. Developed to nurture creativity and enrichment, the fine and performing arts center incorporates both presentation and learning environments for use by the school and surrounding community, including a 400-seat courtyard theater and black box space along with multi-use facilities for such disciplines as 2D/3D graphics, photography and music. Equally important, the airy, spacious and sun-drenched buildings express a unified vision that reduces their impact on the environment, makes efficient use of space, and nurtures a sense of community in a fast-changing world.

Far left: Exterior of Concordia Elementary School

Left: Exterior of the David F. Rittman Performing Arts Center

Above left to right: Arts Center music rehearsal room, elementary school stairway, and Performing Arts theatre

Opposite top: Exterior detail of Concordia elementary school

Photography: Tim Griffith

147

Perkins Eastman

Princeton Day School
Princeton, New Jersey

Top left: Studio

Top right: David Mathey '47 Atrium

Above: Dance studio

Right: Library

Photography: Tom Crane

Less can be more even for a distinguished, independent K-12 school with 900 students occupying a heavily wooded, 105-acre campus in Princeton, New Jersey. Princeton Day School and its architect, Perkins Eastman, have devised a creative alternative to clearing land for new upper school facilities. The 33,000-square-foot renovations and 52,000-square-foot additions to an existing upper school building come at the same time Perkins Eastman has prepared a master plan for the institution, formed by the 1965 merger of a girls' school, Miss Fine's School (1899) and a boys' school, Princeton Country Day School (1924). Changes to the building have produced new facilities for the arts, including studios for ceramics, sculpture, architecture, painting, woodworking and photography, expanded music rooms and state-of-the-art recording studio, new seminar rooms and "smart" rooms for libraries, upgraded indoor athletic locker and meeting space, and a defined main entrance to the school. The renovations and additions are student-friendly, featuring appropriately scaled furnishings, neutral color palette with splashes of accent color, good wayfinding anchored by a circulatory spine, and low- or no-VOC finishes that help preserve indoor air quality. Equally pleasing is the careful integration of new construction with existing facilities and traditions, making everything alumni-friendly as well.

Perkins+Will

Atlanta • Boston • Charlotte • Chicago • Dallas • Dubai • Hartford • Houston
London • Los Angeles • Miami • Minneapolis • New York • Orlando • Research Triangle Park
San Diego • San Francisco • Seattle • Shanghai • Vancouver • Washington, DC
www.perkinswill.com

Perkins+Will

Ohlone Community College Newark
Center for Health Sciences and Technology
Newark, California

Officially named Ohlone College in 1967, the community college serving San Francisco's East Bay region honors the early Ohlone Indians, an agricultural society that inhabited land where the cities of Fremont and Newark now stand—and devoutly believed in conserving the earth. Their philosophy is especially compelling today, as shown by the new, two-floor, 130,000-square-foot Ohlone Community College Newark Center for Health Sciences and Technology,

designed by Perkins+Will. "I want the Ohlone College Newark Center to be used as the model for every campus and education building in California in terms of environmental performance. When someone says it can't be done I'm going to ask: Have you been to Ohlone?" Hon. John Garamendi, Lt. Governor has said. The new college inaugurates an 81-acre campus in Newark to offer vocational programs for health sciences, biotechnology and environmental

studies. Comprising such key elements as classrooms, teaching laboratories, administrative and faculty offices, bookstore, café and learning resource center—separated into science and technology areas yet united around a campus green or Academic Mall—the award-winning, LEED Platinum-certified school exemplifies sustainable design. Not only does the design incorporate such features as a remediated brownfield site, photovoltaic roof panels, geothermal

heating and cooling, high-efficiency lighting, and durable, long-lasting materials that include recycled content, it provides a dynamic, versatile and attractive environment educators can easily modify. In reviewing the project's achievements, Douglas Treadway, former president/superintendent of Ohlone Community College District, declared, "I have been very pleased with the architectural services of Perkins+Will."

Below left: Courtyard with science and technology wings

Below right: Academic Mall

Opposite top, clockwise from left: Main entrance, school grounds, teaching laboratory, specialized classroom

Photography: Bob Canfield

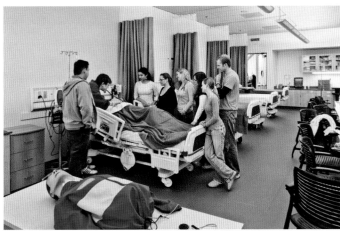

Perkins+Will

Central Middle School
Columbus, Indiana

An inspiring example of how educators are developing innovative teaching methods is the new model being implemented at the two-story, 171,484-square-foot Central Middle School, in Columbus, Indiana. Designed by Perkins+Will as design architect and CSO as architect of record to support small learning communities, the replacement school groups 24 classrooms in "teams" of three classrooms, a science room and shared spaces. By forming small learning communities at the same time the building articulates its massing in team-sized units, the concept turns a larger institution (875 students) into an aggregate of smaller and more responsive ones. Yet, because the building remains flexible in layout, it could easily accommodate a more conventional educational model. The school's creative spirit is also visible elsewhere. For example, the Commons serves as the school's cafeteria and cultural hub, where students can congregate before, during and after classes, and a breakout space for the two adjacent gymnasia. East of the Commons, the Performing Arts area features the "Gray Box" Theater, a multi-purpose venue for stage performances, gatherings and group teaching.

For these and other reasons, district superintendent Dr. John B. Quick recently noted, "This community is blessed with the best middle school in the country."

Top right: Massing of "team" units

Above left: Library

Above right: The Lobby

Right: Exterior with playing field

Opposite: Entrance with canopy-covered walkway

Photography: James Steinkamp

Perkins+Will

Hector P. Garcia Middle School
Dallas, Texas

While every public school represents a vital resource for its community, few are as critical to a constituency far exceeding its own 1,200 students and their families than the new, three-story, 176,000-square-foot Hector P. Garcia Middle School, in Dallas, Texas, designed by Perkins+Will. Compensating for the small land area at nearby W.H. Adamson High School, limited athletic facilities at three neighborhood elementary schools, and lack of community facilities in the north Oak Cliff area, the building offers 27 core academic and special education classrooms, unique, dedicated-use classrooms, library, gymnasium, space for performing and visual arts, 450-seat auditorium, and grounds that include baseball and football fields, running track, and tennis courts. Its progressive outlook, facilitated by floors carefully zoned for shared use, is also manifested in its LEED NC-certified design features. The award-winning school's orientation responds closely to the site's climate and topography. Interior spaces, for example, are set for optimal daylighting that minimizes exposure to Texas' harsh sun. Even the building's compact footprint on the sloping, 13.4-acre site, which leaves the land mostly open for sports activities, boasts water-efficient landscaping that reflects the 10 natural regions of Texas and exceeds the city's storm water protection plan.

Below, top to bottom: North-facing classrooms, main entrance, auditorium

Opposite top left: Cafeteria

Opposite top right: Library

Opposite bottom: Cafeteria seen from outside

Photography: James Steinkamp, Charles Smith (auditorium)

Perkins+Will

**University of Wisconsin Stevens Point
Lee Sherman Dreyfus University Center,
Remodeling and Addition**
Stevens Point, Wisconsin

Above: Concourse with second-floor bridges
Above left: Café lounge
Left: Balcony in Concourse
Below: Remodeled and expanded exterior
Photography: Chris Barrett @ Hedrich Blessing

Free to follow whatever scholarly pursuits interest them, students at the University of Wisconsin Stevens Point all look to the University Centers, namely the Allen Health and Wellness Center, DeBot Residential Dining Center, and Dreyfus University Center, to enrich their campus life. For this reason, the school recently completed a three-level, 149,000-square-foot remodeling and 43,000-square-foot addition to Lee Sherman Dreyfus University Center, designed by Perkins+Will, to encourage attendance and interaction. With new and updated lounges, kitchen and dining, bookstore, ballroom, student services, restaurants, movie theater, night club and offices, the revitalized student union not only expands existing student union offerings, it makes better use of its complex, split-level configuration, using the new Concourse to open up interiors, bridge between levels and permit diagonal circulation. The heightened sense of accessibility comes from the Concourse's clerestory windows on the east and west boundaries and floor-to-ceiling window on the north end, which fill the interior with daylight, and the intimate, glass-enclosed lounges that occupy the interstitial intervals between the Concourse and bookstore, opening up views and focusing attention on the building's multiple levels. Are students finding more room for their friends and interests at Dreyfus? Come join the crowd.

Steven Holl Architects

Steven Holl Architects

University of Iowa
School of Art & Art History, Art Building West
Iowa City, Iowa

Want to experience an extraordinary environment for art students, combining space that is complex, stirring yet user friendly with quality light, modern services and amenities, and a healthy balance between privacy and community? Join the educators calling on a new facility at the University of Iowa. That's right—the University of Iowa, founded in 1847, home of the renowned Iowa Writers' Workshop and world-class research programs in genetics, hydraulics,

and speech and hearing. Pioneering new concepts for art education at its School of Art & Art History and commissioning inspirational architecture for its 1,700-acre campus come naturally to the Iowa City-based institution. The first university to grant credit for creative work in the arts, it startled scholars in the 1930s by combining its art and art history programs into one school. The three-story, 70,000-square-foot Art Building West, designed by Steven Holl Architects as

design architect and Herbert Lewis Kruse Blunck Architecture as architect of record, represents yet another innovation. Encircled by the University's Museum of Art, Art Building and specialized art studios, the Art Build-

Above: Terrace and library overlooking pond

Right: Studio classroom

Opposite: Central atrium

Overleaf: South elevation

Photography: Andy Ryan, Christian Richters

ing West acknowledges its neighbors through compatible scale and massing while taking a radically different approach to planning and design. Steven Holl, a principal of Steven Holl Architects, and his colleagues were inspired by Picasso's 1912 sculpture of a guitar—which explores the instrument's character without replicating it—in conceiving the taut structure of folded and hinged Cor-ten steel plates,

concrete slabs and glass. For this reason, the School's studio classrooms for sculpture, painting and printmaking, graduate studios, faculty and administrative offices, gallery, auditorium, library, meeting rooms and café are arrayed in a decidedly organic configuration. Not only does the structure actively engage such key site features as a quarry pond, limestone bluff and the Art Building, a 1937 brick structure with central

body and flanking wings that stands across the road, it exploits "formless" geometries so its interiors flow into one another and overlap in public areas that act as "social condensers" for people and activities. The result of this conceptual inquiry is startlingly original. Though much of the building wraps around Hutchinson Quarry Pond, the two-floor library, like the neck of a guitar, cantilevers away from the rest of the

Far left: North elevation

Above left: Image archive

Left: Periodical reading room

Opposite top left, right: Auditorium, stack and reading area mass to hover over the water. Inside, the School's activities are informally distributed around a central atrium and its dramatic suspended stair of folded steel plates. Of course, students and faculty are also pleased by the facility's utility. Designed as a working and flexible teaching instrument, the space is flooded with usable light and sweeping vistas that include both the campus outside and activities inside. The facilities are as versatile as they are photogenic, and corridors and stairs offer ample opportunities for social gatherings. In retrospect, the design's understanding of artists should come as no surprise; Steven Holl began his career as a painter. Dorothy Johnson, Carver professor and director of the School of Art & Art History, acknowledged this in declaring, "Students paint, draw, design, photograph and display their art in a work of art, for the architecture itself is sculpted space and light."

Right: Gallery
Below: South elevation

Tai Soo Kim Partners

Tai Soo Kim Partners

Middlebury College
Ross Commons and LaForce Hall
Middlebury, Vermont

A forerunner among institutions in environmental initiatives, Middlebury College advances environmentally responsive design and sustainability in its campus facilities and operations. As a top-tier liberal arts institution founded in 1800 in Middlebury, Vermont, Middlebury serves just 2,350 students, and maintains world-class facilities. Consider Ross Commons, the recently completed 67,000-square-foot residential/dining complex, designed by Tai Soo Kim Partners, comprising a 300-seat, two-story Commons and 67-room, five-story LaForce Hall. Part of Middlebury's new initiative to improve academic, social and residential life on campus, Ross Commons provides a supportive student environment that encourages upperclassmen to live on campus and remain involved in the campus activities, thereby creating a more diverse and balanced social environment for all students. The structures' L-shaped configuration reflect this stewardship, in several aspects: by protecting view corridors of the surrounding Green Mountains with a low profile and transparent building and by forming a quadrangle with adjacent residence halls to increase the sense of a single community of residents. The materials and form of the two structures mirror the barn-like stone architecture found throughout the campus. Equally important, it provides an outstanding living experience. While the Commons features a popular multi-platform servery where fresh food is prepared "exhibition style," LaForce offers a sociable environment of singles and suites with dedicated kitchenettes and bathrooms, as well as a library, seminar and study rooms—making Ross Commons a favorite campus dining and gathering place.

Above: Street view of Commons and LaForce Hall

Left: Fireplace lounge in Commons

Below left: Quadrangle elevations

Below: Seminar room in LaForce Hall

Bottom: Cafeteria

Opposite: Commons servery and dining room

Photography: Timothy Hursley and James Westphalen

Tai Soo Kim Partners

Yale University
Department of Anthropology, 158 Whitney Avenue
New Haven, Connecticut

Although the three-story Greek Revival house at 158 Whitney Avenue in New Haven's historic Hillhouse neighborhood was built as a single-family residence in 1836, the wood-framed structure has spent decades sheltering academic activities. It was acquired by Yale University in 1923 and renovated in 1968 for the Department of Anthropology. Now, following a comprehensive, 12,485-square-foot renovation and 18,100-square-foot addition, designed by Tai Soo Kim Partners, it retains much of its original charm while providing state-of-the-art classrooms, archaeology and dissection laboratories, dry laboratories, conference room, seminar space, faculty offices and workrooms, and administrative offices. Though the construction conscientiously minimizes impact on the historic neighborhood, what looks old isn't necessarily so. Because of the basement's low headroom and moisture problems, the historic building was raised on temporary supports while a new basement level was constructed at a lower elevation as a fully functional space. The addition's stucco and cast stone mask a masonry block wall exploiting a new masonry product made from recycled materials that is light and insulating. The high-tech ventilation control system exhausts laboratory fumes based upon automatic occupancy sensors. After 40 years, 158 Whitney Avenue is a house that finally feels like a home for its anthropologists.

Above: Rear elevation

Above right: Entry lobby

Right: New entrance

Opposite top, clockwise: Administrative offices, seminar space, faculty office, laboratory

Photography: Robert Benson/ Tai Soo Kim

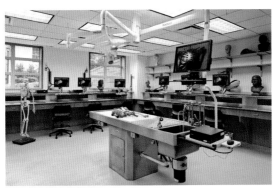

Tai Soo Kim Partners

Bristow Middle School
West Hartford, Connecticut

Envisioned as a "small learning community of choice" drawing its 420 students in grades 6-8 from every neighborhood in West Hartford, Connecticut, the new Bristow Middle School, designed by Tai Soo Kim Partners, has already earned awards from educators and historic preservationists. The project design incorporates a Craftsman-style residential structure designed by Edward T. Hapgood in 1900 situated on a 5.4 acre tree-lined street within a historic district. The historic house—which remains standing after the removal of various additions and new structures erected over the years—makes a major contribution by providing the school's media center, small group instruction facilities and administrative offices within its 12,000-square foot renovated space. Meant for regular use by teachers and students, it connects directly to the new construction by means of a glass passageway that continues through the school as the main corridor. The new three-story, 72,000-square-foot main building is cast in stone, steel, aluminum and glass, in form and colors which complement the stucco, wood and brownstone of the historic structure. The new construction contains the bulk of the school, providing a gymnasium, cafeteria, music and art rooms, a 300-seat auditorium with proscenium and 20 classrooms configured into clusters to facilitate team teaching, fostering a sense of community. Named for a Civil War era slave who purchased his freedom and became a respected agricultural expert in Hartford, the Bristow School also accommodates

Top: Cafeteria

Above: Auditorium with proscenium

Right: The Shepard House on the Bristow campus

Opposite: Main corridor

Photography: Paul Warchol and Tai Soo Kim

Tai Soo Kim Partners

Below: Science classroom
Right: Main entrance
Bottom: Atrium at main entrance

environmental concerns. Numerous "green" design measures, such as making daylight an integral part of the lighting design to conserve energy, employing low-E glass, overhangs and sunscreens to reduce heat gain, and developing a compact building plan to protect open space, help to optimize the school's performance. One feature has proven to be as effective as it is invisible, at least from the street. The new 17,000-square-foot parking is situated underground, eliminating one potential obstacle in integrating the school into its historic, tree-lined district.

VOA Associates Incorporated

VOA Associates Incorporated

Rose-Hulman Institute of Technology
Hatfield Hall
Terre Haute, Indiana

What attracts 1,900 talented undergraduates annually to Rose-Hulman Institute of Technology, in Terre Haute, Indiana? Rose-Hulman is one of America's best colleges of engineering, science and mathematics, top rated in its category by *U.S. News & World Report* ten years in a row. At the same time, the college founded in 1874 as the Rose Polytechnic Institute encourages its students to broaden their intellectual horizons. That's why a striking new, two-story, 49,500-square-foot modern facility, Hatfield Hall, designed by VOA Associates, recently appeared on the 295-acre campus, combining a performing arts center with the college's development office. Hatfield Hall supports the performing arts with a 600-seat theater with proscenium stage and orchestra pit, drama and music rehearsal rooms, music practice rooms, green room, scene shop, offices and gathering spaces. To help it serve the development office, the design pairs a soaring, two-story, glass-enclosed pre-function room, which gives the theater a grand public image, with a smaller but more formal "alumni room," a buffer for the development office that serves as a multi-purpose space for housing important alumni documents, honoring school benefactors, and hosting high-level dinners and other special events whenever Rose-Hulman wants to put on a show.

Top: Alumni room
Above: Theater
Left: Exterior
Opposite: Pre-function room
Photography: James Steinkamp

VOA Associates Incorporated

Fairmont State University
Falcon Center
Fairmont, West Virginia

Since student life extends well beyond the classroom and laboratory, Fairmont State University, in Fairmont, West Virginia, has just given its 4,600 students enticing new opportunities to connect with each other, faculty and staff on its 120-acre main campus by opening the three-story, 146,500-square-foot Falcon Center, designed by VOA Associates. Falcon Center, an award-winning blend of new construction with adaptive re-use of an adjacent structure, appeals to a wide spectrum of students by recognizing their diversity of interests. It consists of a recreation center, featuring two gymnasiums with basketball, volleyball, soccer, tennis and badminton courts. It also includes a running track, fitness center, and indoor leisure pool as well as incorporating a dining hall, conference center, multipurpose rooms, bookstore, administrative offices, game room, convenience store and café. It is a forward-looking facility in many ways. It restricts its footprint and profile, for example, to nestle gently into the West Virginia foothills. A centrally positioned circulation spine and atrium dubbed "Main Street" allows for views of all three floors, a design that helps create unity. The intention was to bring together the student body; no matter what activity they are engaged in, they are all experiencing the same thing. Though its development preceded LEED certification, Falcon Center promotes a healthy environment through natural ventilation, generous daylight, and low-VOC product specifications for interior finishes so that a university founded in 1865 remains as lively as its students.

Above left: Exterior
Top right: Atrium
Above right: Dining hall
Right: Fitness center
Opposite: Circulation spine
Photography: Christopher Barrett/Hedrich Blessing

VOA Associates Incorporated

Kennedy-King College
Chicago, Illinois

No less than legendary attorney Clarence Darrow defended the City Colleges of Chicago during the Depression, arguing that the junior colleges (converted to comprehensive community colleges in 1966) were indispensable as higher education "for the people." A resounding affirmation of Darrow's faith, Kennedy-King College, now thrives at a brand-new campus. Occupying 18 acres on Chicago's South Side, the new six-building, 467,000-square-foot campus—founded in 1935 as Woodrow Wilson Junior College and renamed in 1969 to honor Robert F.

Kennedy and Martin Luther King Jr.—simultaneously offers a broad curriculum and revitalizes a struggling neighborhood. Its award-winning master plan and design, by Kennedy-King Architects LLC, a joint venture of VOA Associates and Johnson & Lee, Ltd Architects/Planners, enables the school to escape the limitations of its previous one-building facility and expand its services to the public. The complex replaces a declining commercial district with brick-clad buildings oriented around a green quadrangle with a clock tower and offers efficient, state-of-the-art facilities featuring generous

windows and well-coordinated finishes. Through its classrooms, library, laboratories, TV/radio studios, theater and offices to sports facilities, bookstore, cafeteria and student center, Kennedy-King College has brought new life and new hope to a grateful community.

Top: Campus quadrangle with clock tower
Above right: Natural science classroom
Right: Washburne Culinary Institute
Below right: Natatorium
Opposite: Entrance
Photography: Ballogg Photography

VOA Associates Incorporated

University of Notre Dame
Mendoza College of Business, Executive MBA
Chicago, Illinois

Corporate executives in Chicago earning an Executive MBA from Notre Dame's Mendoza College of Business, based in South Bend, Indiana, have discovered how to be in two places at once. Notre Dame's Executive MBA program recently joined forces with the University Development office and Alumni Club of Chicago to develop and share a versatile new, one-floor, 10,000-square-foot facility, designed by VOA Associates, in Chicago's historic Santa Fe Building. The facility, comprising a reception area, classroom, breakout rooms, office support room, service kitchen and multi-purpose room for dining, receptions, meetings and seminars, is well equipped for its mission. An unmistakable visual identity is created for Notre Dame by incorporating visual cues to the school's traditional set-tings in the colors, finishes, millwork and furniture of the reception area, which faces the historic atrium. The classroom, by contrast, locates its modern forms, finishes, lighting, A/V equipment and other technology support away from the atrium at a busy urban intersection. Special attention was paid to room acoustics both in the placement of mechanical equipment and attentuation of noise from the street and atrium. Sharon Keane, Mendoza's co-director of executive education, praises the design for respecting history "while augmenting it with a first-rate learning environment that meets the unique needs of executive students." Indeed, it's the second facility for Mendoza designed by VOA, which prides itself on knowing what business wants.

Top left: Tiered classroom
Top right: Multipurpose room
Above: View from building atrium
Photography: Charlie Mayer

Yost Grube Hall Architecture

Yost Grube Hall Architecture

Oregon State University
Kelley Engineering Center
Corvallis, Oregon

A passion for research has shaped Oregon State University from its founding in 1858, and continues to inspire renowned programs involving such fields as engineering, environmental sciences, forestry and pharmacy. One of OSU's newest research facilities is the 153,000-square-foot Kelley Engineering Center designed by Yost Grube Hall Architecture. The project eloquently illustrates how research is evolving and expressed on its 400-acre campus in Corvallis. To encourage 320 students and 140 faculty members to socialize and exchange ideas, the building organizes classrooms, breakout spaces, research laboratories, computer laboratory and administrative offices in three- and four-story rectangular volumes flanking the north and south sides of a central atrium. The atrium nurtures collaborative activity through six bridges crossing its main axis, a central stairway, spacious balcony and ground-level café. Not only is seating available throughout the atrium, convenient places for casual encounters can also be found where hallways intersect. More subtly, the design nurtures interaction and expresses the mission by providing a sustainable, LEED Gold-certified environment featuring daylight, natural ventilation, water conservation, energy efficiency and other green measures. Ron Adams, OSU's dean of engineering, notes that the Center has "...met or exceeded our expectations in its ability to foster collaboration and serve our students' learning and our faculty's research."

Above left: Arcade in central atrium

Above: Central atrium

Left: Flexible study space

Below: Exterior, northwest corner

Opposite: Exterior view of atrium west elevation

Photography: Peter Eckert

Yost Grube Hall Architecture

Humboldt State University
Behavioral and Social Sciences Building
Arcata, California

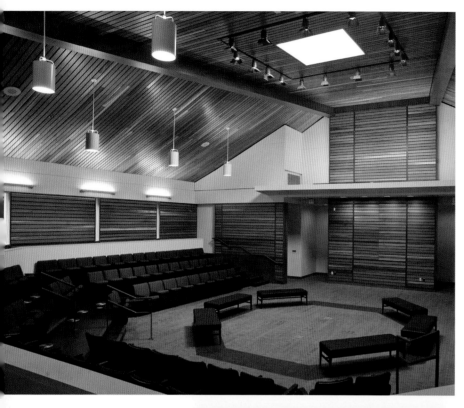

Above: Amphitheater-style lecture hall

Above right: Northwest approach to building

Right: View of complex's five-story and one-story structures

Below right: Classroom

Opposite: View of building from southeast

Photography: Peter Eckert

In a residential neighborhood of Arcata, California, Humboldt State University has successfully completed the 90,500-square-foot Behavioral and Social Sciences Building designed by Yost Grube Hall Architecture. The building's complex program is comprised of faculty and departmental offices, lecture halls and classrooms, as well as specialized areas such as an intercultural communications forum. The building also accommodates California State University's Center for Native American Studies, Humboldt's anthropology department, psychology clinic and world language and culture teaching laboratories. Neighborhood support for the project was gained with a reduction in scale by breaking the scheme into two structures of one and five stories, and a site plan positioning the lower building on the residential street and the higher one further back, behind existing trees and perpendicular to the street. The building's interiors are handled with equal skill. Students, faculty and the Native American regional tribes and communities served by the Center enjoy a LEED Gold-certified interior environment incorporating such features as daylight, natural ventilation and reclaimed rainwater. The excellence of the design caused Traci Ferdolage, Humboldt's project manager, to declare, "We are very proud of both buildings designed by Yost Grube Hall."

Yost Grube Hall Architecture

Portland Community College
Cascade Campus Master Plan and Buildings
Portland, Oregon

Can an educational institution expand in a tight urban location, between a commercially zoned area and a residential area, to develop a campus with a genuine sense of place while maintaining the support of local business people and homeowners? Though this scenario is not uncommon for urban colleges, the award-winning solution for the Cascade Campus of Portland Community College, involving a master plan and buildings designed by Yost Grube Hall Architecture, could inspire educators everywhere.

To win the trust of area residents, the college opened communications with the Neighborhood Association, drafting a "good neighbor agreement" to ensure they would have a voice in its expansion. The college also used Portland's flexible new land use tool, the Impact Mitigation Plan, to assess the potential future impact for all buildings and describe plans for mitigating it. As a result, the existing four-building campus is making better use of open and underused parcels, strengthening its border on the commercial district with storefront-style façades, opening a large plaza and quadrangle along a central green spine in the heart of campus. The plan renovates existing buildings and develops new ones that complement both their commercial and residential counterparts—a good neighbor on and off campus.

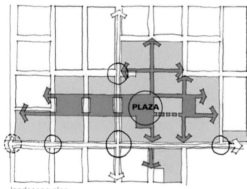
landscape plan

Top right, left and below: New and remodeled buildings on campus

Above right: Central green spine of landscape plan

Right: Major pedestrian traffic in circulation plan

Photography: Peter Eckert

Illustration: Courtesy of Yost Grube Hall Architecture

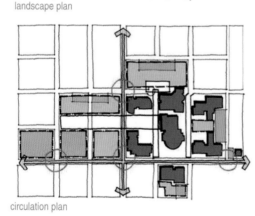
circulation plan

Yost Grube Hall Architecture

Portland State University
Academic and Student Recreation Center
Portland, Oregon

"Fusion" buildings combining multiple complex programmatic elements are increasingly serving school campuses for reasons of economy, efficiency and synergy. Consider the new, six-story, 200,000-square-foot Academic and Student Recreation Center at Portland State University, in Portland, Oregon, designed by Yost Grube Hall Architecture. When completed, the building will bring many vital functions to a confined, full block site in downtown Portland. The building will help define the existing Urban Plaza with a façade that showcases internal activities and relates to the façades of nearby buildings, as well as preside as the urban center for the school's campus. To thicken the plot, the building will reconcile the 13-ft. site gradient by installing entries to its lobby on two levels and retail entries at six different elevations. Clearly, the Center is a richly complex facility. However, building users will have no trouble finding the Student Recreation Center's three-court gymnasium, multi-purpose group fitness rooms, elevated running track, lap swimming pool and whirlpool spa, climbing wall, cardiovascular and free weights area and locker rooms; or the facility's classrooms, 2,500-seat lecture hall, School of Social Work, chancellor's office and City of Portland Archives. Notes Alex Accetta, PSU's director of campus recreation, "Yost Grube Hall has taken good care of us."

Above: Façade facing Urban Plaza

Right: Three-court gymnasium

Below right: Cardio and weights

Below: Exterior viewed from Urban Plaza

Illustration: Courtesy of Yost Grube Hall Architecture

Yost Grube Hall Architecture

University of Botswana
Master Plan
Gaborone, Botswana

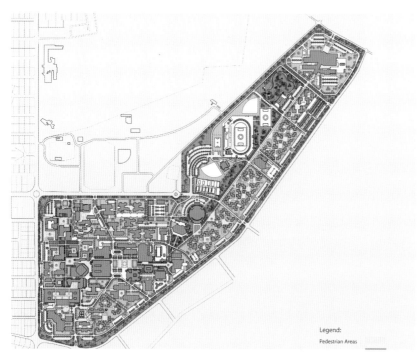

Legend:
Pedestrian Areas

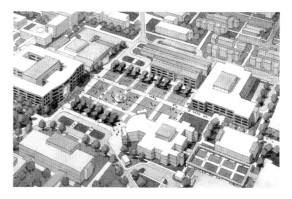

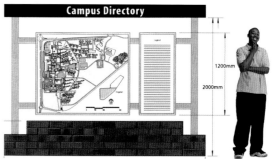

Campus Directory

1200mm

2000mm

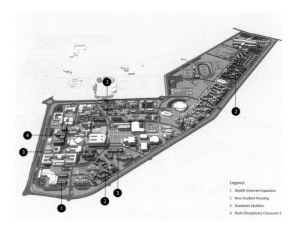

Legend:
1. Health Sciences Expansion
2. New Student Housing
3. Academic Facilities
4. Multi-Disciplinary Classroom E

Although the University of Botswana was established in 1982, its origin traces to the opening of the University of Basutoland, Bechuanaland and Swaziland in 1964. Much has changed since then, as the university attained its current enrollment of 15,500 students. Yost Grube Hall Architecture's work on the University of Botswana's new 2009-2016 and Beyond Master Plan is but the latest step in their relationship. The University's 2001 Master Plan, also completed by Yost Grube Hall Architecture in collaboration with Botswana's FMA Architects, defined campus facility requirements and established a planning framework to expand enrollment from 10,000 to 15,000. Subsequently, the architect provided programming services for over 700,000 square feet of new construction, and worked on two current campus facility projects with FMA Architects. Today, the new Master Plan defines the facility requirements and campus planning framework to serve over 20,000 students with an increased focus on graduate study and research. Developing siting concepts for the majority of new construction, the plan also outlines a framework for facility, open-space, landscape and sustainability design standards. The Master Plan for the 284-acre Gaborone campus is certainly ambitious, but the University of Botswana aspires to be nothing less than a leading world center of educational excellence.

Top left: Pedestrian open space plan

Above: Central plaza concept view

Middle: Signage standards development

Below: Phased facility development plan

Illustration: Martin Milward (top right); Courtesy of Yost Grube Hall Architecture (top left, above middle and above)

Lighting

Lighting

Let there be light: Educators and the architects, planners and designers who serve them know the importance of lighting in education. Since education is now recognized as key to America's wellbeing, increasingly sophisticated and highly specialized physical environments to support learning are showing up across the country where lighting is a critical component of the architecture and interior design. Think of the many ways illumination helps differentiate the educational world by age groups, learning methodologies and activities, times of day and year, and so forth, turning spaces into clasassrooms, laboratories, libraries and dormitories, to name a handful of educational building types. The lighting design firms featured in the following pages illustrate how vast the opportunities are for quality lighting in education.

SBLD Studio

SBLD Studio

Adventure Science Center and Sudekum Planetarium
Nashville, Tennessee

Left: Exhibit hall and pyramidal roof

Bottom left: Space Walker is visible to passersby

Bottom right: Entrance to Solar System Survey

Opposite: Worlds of Wonder projects 360° images of sun, planets and moons

Photography: ©Albert Vecerka/Esto

Children have delighted in Nashville's Adventure Science Center and Sudekum Planetarium since it opened as the Children's Museum of Nashville in 1944. Now, with the completion of a spectacular two-level, 38,000-square-foot addition for a new planetarium and planetarium offices, exhibit hall and public spaces, designed by Tuck Hinton Architects, architect, Ralph Appelbaum Associates, exhibit designer and SBLD Studio, lighting designer, they have many more reasons to visit. Inspired by the Pyramids and Stonehenge as ancient celestial timepieces, the design team has created a compelling interactive environment that welcomes over 260,000 children and more than a few adults annually to such exhibits as the Solar System Survey, Planet Walk, Worlds of Wonder, Testbed and the 166-seat, 63-foot diameter Planetarium, where an integrated optical star projector displays 6.5 million stars. The building's distinctive architectural envelope is supported everywhere by theatrical lighting effects. The color-changing pyramidal roof, for example, is now a Nashville icon. Ambient illumination of the Space Walker display directly behind the exhibit hall's curtain wall turns it into a living theater. And dramatic illumination using saturated color, floating LED lines and gobo projections brings feature exhibits to light while keeping visitors young and old happily in the dark.

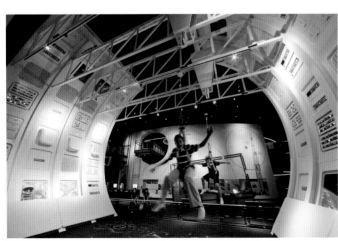

SBLD Studio

United States Military Academy
Thomas Jefferson Hall Library and Learning Center
West Point, New York

History's shadows stretch across the lawns of the United States Military Academy, in West Point, New York, where the roster of graduates reaching back to 1802 includes such leaders as Grant, Lee, Pershing, MacArthur, Eisenhower, Patton, Schwarzkopf and Petraeus. That's why the new six-story, 151,000-square-foot Thomas Jefferson Hall Library and Learning Center, designed by STV Group with Holzman Moss Architecture, architects, and SBLD Studio, lighting designer, honors the past as it explores the future. The first new academic building in the central campus in over 35 years, Jefferson Hall houses the Cadet Library's collections area—containing 500,000 books—along with a reading and group study area, meeting rooms and library support area, Center for Teaching Excellence and Center for Enhanced Performance in settings ranging from informal gathering spaces to technology-rich classrooms and interactive learning facilities. The lighting design is appropriately based on a pallet blending modern lighting technologies with an aesthetic reflecting West Point's Collegiate Gothic tradition. Custom fixtures pair energy-efficient lamp

technologies with standard products to create uniform solutions blending seamlessly with the building and campus. Like the building's wireless Internet and sophisticated audiovisual equipment, the lighting is unobtrusive but ready to serve West Point in its third century.

Above left: Lobby
Above: Reading area
Left: Exterior
Photography: Tom Kessler

SBLD Studio

Columbia University Teachers College
The Gottesman Libraries, Millbank Memorial Library
New York, New York

With its tradition of innovation and insights, Teachers College at Columbia University, in New York City, is one of the country's leading schools of education. As part of extensive efforts to restore the splendor of Teachers College and update its facilities for modern scholarship and technology, the 53,430-square-foot Millbank Memorial Library, part of the famed Gottesman Libraries and one of America's finest research libraries in education, has been transformed into a 21st-century facility by Shepley Bulfinch Richardson Abbott, in association with FXFOWLE Architects, and SBLD Studio, lighting designer. The construction gives the library such new and refurbished facilities as compact stacks, study carrels, central service desk, information commons, classrooms with adjacent breakout rooms, collaborative study areas, media laboratories, grand reading room,and a café. Because of previous remodeling, the rehabilitation evokes the library's historic nature rather than its original form, so the lighting design incorporates current lighting level standards, modern lamp sources, and energy-efficient design concepts. Custom-designed lighting fixtures are skillfully integrated with standard lighting products to meet a tight budget, conserve energy and portray Millbank's glorious space in its best light.

SBLD Studio

Vanderbilt University
Buttrick Hall
Nashville, Tennessee

Consistently ranked as one of America's top 20 universities by *U.S. News & World Report*, Vanderbilt University attracts some 11,500 students annually to Nashville, where it conducts cutting-edge research within Neoclassical and Collegiate Gothic buildings. This flair for balancing new and old recently resulted in the transformation of Buttrick Hall, an imposing 1927 brick-and-stone structure once slated for demolition, into a center for such interdisciplinary programs as Film Studies, Jewish Studies and the Curb Center for Art, Enterprise, and Public Policy. With Tuck Hinton Architects as architect and SBLD as lighting designer, the five-level, 90,950-square-foot facility (including a 49,650-square-foot addition)

has been given new lecture halls, private meeting rooms, movie theater, offices and a central atrium that integrates the building's old and new sections. The lighting design creatively highlights and articulates architectural details while giving individual spaces the special attention they require. In the atrium, for example, daylight is supplemented by concealed asymmetrical fluorescent uplights and wall-mounted metal halide can fixtures. At the main entry, metal halide floodlights highlight the entry arch while an overhead fixture brightens the doorway. For a building once considered obsolete, Buttrick Hall now glows with vitality.

Above: Atrium

Top right: Main entry

Photography: Rion Rizzo/Creative Sources

SBLD Studio

Belmont University
Beaman Student Life Center and Curb Event Center
Nashville, Tennessee

One of the nation's fastest-growing Christian universities with nearly 4,800 students coming from almost every state and over two dozen countries, Nashville's Belmont University strives to enhance the student experience inside and outside the classroom on its 75-acre campus. Opened in September 2003, the two-story, 220,000-square-foot Beaman Student Life Center and Curb Event Center was designed by Earl Swensson Associates, architect, and SBLD Studio, lighting designer. The facility's Neo-classical architecture, inspired by the antebellum Italianate Belmont Mansion (1852) that anchored the former Belle Monte estate and remains a campus landmark today, Responding to students' social and recreational interests, the Beaman Center offers lounges and meeting rooms, game room, student government offices, juice bar, student-managed retail space, coffee shop, fitness center, intramural gymnasium, indoor racquetball courts, aerobics and weight rooms, 36-foot rock-climbing wall and 5,000-seat arena. The lighting design assiduously supports the numerous specialized accommodations that make the Centers so appealing, providing warmth and intimacy to smaller and more contemplative spaces, reinforcing the drama and expansiveness in larger and more dynamic areas, and brightening student life overall on the Belmont campus.

Top left: Exterior with fountain courtyard
Top right: Chandelier
Left: Atrium lounge
Photography: Attila Uysal

SBLD Studio

Syracuse University
Martin J. Whitman School of Management
Syracuse, New York

How would students respond to a building designed from the ground up as a student-focused, high-tech facility that supports the learning experiences essential to a world-class management education within a community-oriented environment? Ask students at Syracuse University's Martin J. Whitman School of Management, who recently moved into the six-story, 160,000-square-foot facility, designed by FXFOWLE Architects, architect, and SBLD Studio, lighting designer. Every design decision was made with these goals in mind. Among the building's extensive facilities are 22 classrooms, 20 team meeting rooms each for undergraduate and graduate students, computer clusters, 200-seat auditorium, 74 faculty offices, faculty research center, investment research center, center for entrepreneurial start-ups, 100-seat café, special events room with outdoor terrace, and a spectacular, glass-sheathed,

three-story, 4,000-square-foot Grand Hall. Interestingly, since the school is strategically located to be a prominent campus gateway, its lighting design serves both building occupants and campus pedestrians. On campus, the glow from within the Grand Hall and circulation spine creates a lantern-like beacon that helps link surrounding campus sites. Inside, the lighting addresses such issues as energy efficiency, flexibility, multi-tiered controls and ease of maintenance, providing the school an empirical lesson in green design.

Top: Exterior
Above: Grand Hall
Left: Café
Lower left: Corridor
Photography: ©Jeff Goldberg/Esto

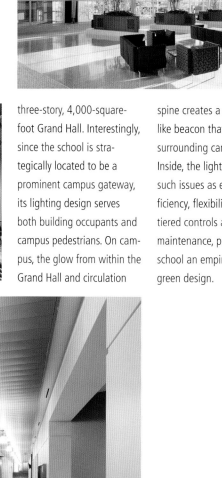

Schuler Shook

Theatre Planners • Architectural Lighting Designers

750 North Orleans, Suite 400 • Chicago, IL 60654 • 312.944.8230 • (F) 312.944.8297

123 Third Street North, Suite 210 • Minneapolis, MN 55401 • 612.339.5958 • (F) 612.337.5097

302 North Market Street, Suite 500 • Dallas, TX 75202 • 214.747.8300 • (F) 214.747.8400

www.schulershook.com

Schuler Shook Theatre Planners

Detroit School of Arts
Detroit, Michigan

Right: Orchestra rehearsal room

Far right: Auditorium

Below and below right: Black box theatre and dance studio

Bottom: Exterior at night

Photography: Curt Clayton, SECOA (proscenium theatre)

City dwellers know it's often easier to find space by reaching vertically rather than horizontally. Making this concept work was a major challenge for the new, six-floor, 300,000-square-foot Detroit School of Arts and its narrow 2.5-acre site in Detroit. Designed by Hamilton Anderson Associates as architect with Schuler Shook as theatre consultants, the school features various performance spaces, including an 800-seat auditorium with full working stage and pit lift as well as two balconies, a 200-seat recital hall, a 150-seat black box theatre with galleries and catwalks, two television studios sized 3,000 square feet and 5,000 square feet, three dance rehearsal rooms, and orchestra, band and choral rehearsal rooms. To overcome spatial constraints, the design connects performance and production facilities by stacking them, and provides large corridors and freight elevators to transport scenic units and technical equipment. It's one of numerous measures—the school is LEED Certified, for example—in an ambitious project that also houses the new Communications Production Center for Detroit Public Television and the new radio facility for WDTR-FM, the Detroit Public Schools radio station. Of course, what the 1,200 students want is to put on a great show, and that's how this school excels.

Schuler Shook Lighting Designers

Valparaiso University
Christopher Center for Library and Information Resources
Valparaiso, Indiana

Since the tumultuous changes wrought by information technologies and educational policies continue to reshape the nation's schools, Valparaiso University is not alone in wanting its new library, the four-floor, 115,000-square-foot Christopher Center for Library and Information Resources, to keep its options open. The need for a superior environment that remains flexible for future reconfiguration has nevertheless resulted in an outstanding facility, designed by EHDD as architect and Schuler Shook as lighting designer. In fact, the building's accommodations, including reading rooms, stacks, classrooms, writing centers, conference room, computer laboratories, community room, lounges and café, have made it a superb research center and favored gathering place on Valparaiso's 310-acre campus in Valparaiso, Indiana. The lighting design helps the building respond to current and future conditions. Not only does it conserve energy by utilizing energy-efficient, long-lasting lamps, it provides warm, quality light using direct and indirect fixtures that allow the stacks and other elements to easily be reconfigured. Its impact is keenly felt at night. Knowing the building would be a visible landmark after dark, the design team took care to adjust colors, finishes and lighting to let the interior glow like a welcoming lantern to some 4,000 undergraduate and graduate students.

Below left: Mezzanine, grand stair and reading room
Below center: Reading room
Below right: Conference room
Bottom: Exterior at night
Opposite top: Stacks and lounge
Photography: Peter Aaron/ Esto

Schuler Shook Lighting Designers

Minneapolis Community & Technical College Library and Parking Ramp
Minneapolis, Minnesota

Minnesota's tenth largest post-secondary educational institution, Minneapolis Community & Technical College, gets down to business quickly, providing 11,000 students annually with such basic services as technical education, workforce development, English language learning and continuing education. Fortunately, its practicality doesn't exclude good design on campus. New lighting for the library and parking ramp, designed by Schuler Shook, gives students exceptional environments that conserve energy, extend lamp life and raise the school's public image. For the new three-story, 64,000-square-foot library and instructional technology facility, designed by Cuningham Group as architect, Schuler Shook created lighting for settings as varied as reading rooms, stacks, study areas and resource rooms, highlighted by perimeter up/down illumination at the soffit level on each floor. The perimeter scheme produces a sleek luminous band that is visible inside and outside. Because previous lighting for the parking ramp at the entry to the campus was uninviting and ignored the opportunity to establish a campus gateway, the design team of Bentz/Thompson/Rietow as architect and Schuler Shook as lighting designer introduced an uplighted array of bar grating columns, each topped by an etched glass disk, flanked by perforated metal panels. The lighting of the ramp's façade, paralleled by the library across the street, provides the campus identity and western entry to Downtown Minneapolis.

Right: Library perimeter lighting
Below left: Illuminated wall at parking ramp
Below: Detail of wall's columns and panels
Photography: Daryl Pratte (library), Philip Prowse Photography (parking ramp)

Schuler Shook Theatre Planners • Lighting Designers

Mississippi State University
Riley Center
Meridian, Mississippi

The future looked bright for Meridian, Mississippi when I. Marks and his half-brother Levi Rothenberg built the Grand Opera House and Marks Rothenberg department store side by side. In 1889, Meridian seemed to be a strategic railroad stop between New Orleans and Chicago, and the men were anxious to promote culture as well as invest wisely. A century later, their vision shimmers in an award-winning restoration, designed by Martinez & Johnson Architecture as architect and Schuler Shook as theatre consultant and lighting designer, that gives Mississippi State University the Riley Center, a performing arts and conference center and prime down- town location. Ironically, the closing of the Opera House in 1927, hurt by the rise of movie theatres, facilitated its rebirth. Entangled in lawsuits for decades, the building was left untouched, making historic restoration possible. However, the 950-seat facility needed modern additions. The third-floor stagehouse, for example, required a raised roof to accommodate modern scenery rigging. Space was appropriated from neighboring buildings to enlarge the small stage. None of the original light fixtures remained, so new replicas were fabricated. Consequently, when the curtain rises at the Riley Center, the experience remains grand— or even grander.

Above: Stage view of orchestra, first and second balconies

Right: Orchestra seating

Below: Proscenium seen from first balcony

Photography: Whitney Cox

Schuler Shook Lighting Designers

University of Minnesota
McNamara Alumni Center
Minneapolis, Minnesota

For years, alumni of the University of Minnesota have longed for a place of their own on the Minneapolis campus, a virtual "front door" surrounded by some 70,000 students, faculty members and staff. Thanks to generous alumni and three building owners, they can now gather at the new, six-story, 231,000-square- foot McNamara Alumni Center, the first facility of its kind since the university's founding in 1851. The building is unusual in other ways. Its volume is divided into a 38,000-square-foot public space on the first floor for alumni and 193,000- square-foot office space on the second through sixth floors for commercial tenants inside a striking, granite-covered "geode" designed by the renowned Antoine Predock as design architect, KKE Architects as executive architect, and Schuler Shook as lighting designer. The lighting helps the building command attention wherever one views it. For example, the main hall uses theatrical accent lights, floor uplights, and recessed adjustable fixtures to give its dramatically angled wood surfaces a warm radiance visible from far away. Elsewhere inside and outside, a variety of fixtures and a minimal number of energy- saving, long-life luminaires are employed to support the functional requirements of the center and assure alumni that they are truly "home" with alma mater.

Below left: Main entrance doorway

Below: Skylights in the main hall

Bottom left: Arch from historic stadium that occupied site

Photography: Timothy Hursley

Wayfinding

Wayfinding

Can't you read the sign? By the time someone says that, we're lost. Way-finding is a common issue today because our complex, diverse, mobile and changing society keeps redefining itself, leaving many of us confused and disoriented along the way. But wayfinding is about orientation on many levels, as students, faculty, alumni and visitors to today's educational facilities know first-hand. So we look to signs for campus maps, building floor plans, building identification, directions, information, individual room identification and regulatory notices. In recent years, we have also started regarding signs as branding symbols, identifying large, complicated and physically dispersed aggregates of land and buildings as elements of the same institution. The wayfinding firms featured in the following pages show how today's education finds its way.

Biesek Design

Biesek Design

University of Southern California
Edward L. Doheny Memorial Library
Los Angeles, California

Though Los Angeles was still a frontier town when the University of Southern California opened its doors in 1880, the school completed its first freestanding library and one of the most important and popular facilities on campus, the Edward L. Doheny Memorial Library, designed by Samuel Lunden, just a half century later in 1932. Revered as the library is, its learning environment provides state-of-the-art spaces for studying, collaborative work and special events as well as a vast book and periodical collection. The seven-story, 167,000-square-foot Romanesque Revival structure, which has a five-story perimeter and seven-story stack at its core, recently unveiled a comprehensive historic wayfinding and signage program, designed by Biesek Design, to bring its circulation plans up to date. While interior and exterior signage echoes the library's historic architecture, their materials and methods are quite contemporary. Signs were cast in glass fiber reinforced plaster (GFRP), coated with bronze and finished in a classic, statuary luster. Now that the sign system planning, design, and construction have given way to an unobtrusive yet strategically positioned signage system that feels simultaneously timeless and user friendly, new generations of students and faculty will have no difficulty exploring Doheny Memorial's rich resources.

Below left: Main Directory sign

Below: The Feuchtwanger Memorial Library, a special Collection

Top, left to right, top to bottom: Main entrance, Stacks sign, Entry lunette panel and original signage, new directional and floor plan orientation signs

Photography: John Livzey, Jim Simmons, Jack Biesek

Biesek Design

University of California, Los Angeles
Campus Signage Master Plan
Los Angeles, California

Below: Entrance to Royce Hall displaying new signature lettering

Right: Exterior sign for handicapped users

Below left: Exterior building identification sign

Below right: New carved building signature lettering

Opposite top, left to right: Gateway entry sign, pedestrian map

Photography: Barry Goyette, Jack Biesek

College campuses resemble self-contained cities in many ways. Consider the 419-acre campus of the University of California, Los Angeles in the Westwood district. Some 39,000 students study here with over 4,000 faculty members, going back and forth among some 174 buildings that function as classroom buildings, libraries, laboratories, sports facilities, performing arts venues, student residences, healthcare facilities and more. To give the campus wayfinding system a single, dependable and immediately recognizable voice, Biesek Design has created a new campus wayfinding and signage master plan. The comprehensive program encompasses interior and exterior signage, sign standards for roadway, pedestrian and architectural applications, and collaboration on facility development with such renowned architects as Robert Venturi and Denise Scott Brown, Moore, Ruble, Yudell, Cesar Pelli, and Perkins+Will. Featuring a unique typeface created by Biesek Design called UCLA Gothic, the new, ADA-compliant design standards are distributed to consulting campus architects to produce signage ranging from signature lettering on each building that is carved into stone or fabricated in metal to more typical signs for such sites as classrooms, pedestrian paths and parking structures. To date, the ongoing implementation program (1993 to 2009) has produced over 30,000 signs bearing the new look.

Biesek Design

California Polytechnic State University
Christopher Cohan Center
San Luis Obispo, California

"Cal Poly" or California Poly-technic State University at San Luis Obispo and the City of San Luis Obispo scored a satisfying win-win by build-ing the dynamic Christopher Cohan Center, designed by Daniel, Mann, Johnson & Mendenhall and Alberto Bertoli, AIA (Warnecke & Associates). Developed by the partnership of Cal Poly, the city and the Founda-tion for the Performing Arts Center, the state-of-the-art facility for the perform-ing arts serves the greater community as well as the campus, accomplishing what

none of the partners could do alone. The building's com-position reflects its complex sponsorship, incorporating the existing 498-seat Alex and Faye Spanos Theatre in a larger structure that includes a 1,289-seat concert hall, 180-seat recital hall and the Pavilion, a multi-purpose venue. Biesek Design's contri-bution to this effort was to plan, design and implement all signage, including the creation of an innovative technique to display donor recognition graphics in a meaningful, contemporary way. While the entire signage

program proved highly suc-cessful, the donor recognition graphics drew particular attention. Etched on floor-to-ceiling crystal glass sheets illuminated by fiber-optic lighting, the names of the hundreds of donors to the new facility appear to float in mid-air. It's a dazzling vi-sion to accompany stunning architecture.

Right: Exterior

Below: Entrance to Ticket Office

Below right: Donor recognition graphics

Opposite below, left to right, top to bottom: Close up of typeface, interior of concert hall, sign for hearing impaired, close-up of Ticket Office sign.

Photography: Barry Goyette, Jack Biesek

Biesek Design

University of California, Santa Barbara
Mosher Alumni Center
Santa Barbara, California

Sometimes simplicity produces the best design solutions, as can be seen in the comprehensive wayfinding signage and donor recognition graphics program for the new Mosher Alumni Center at the University of California, Santa Barbara. The three-story, 14,000-square-foot Mosher Alumni House, designed by noted architect and UCSB alumnus Barry Berkus, is a highly visible destination for returning graduates seeking to renew their association with the campus and participate in alumni activities. As a gathering place for alumni and their families, it provides comfortable meeting facilities, outdoor terraces, galleries and a library to make former students feel at home once more on campus. Biesek Design worked closely with campus planners and facility operations staff as well as the Alumni Association to implement a signage program that echoed elements of the building's architecture and finishes. While simple solutions employing dimensional letters, green glass (acrylic) sign panels and complementary colors helped the signage blend into the building décor, such traditional and venerable material finishes as bronze, stainless steel and glass gave the donor recognition graphics the respect they deserved. The result is an environment where the support of alumni for their alma mater is visible in a subtle yet flattering way.

Poulin + Morris Inc.

Poulin + Morris Inc.

University of Pennsylvania
Wharton School of Business, Jon M. Huntsman Hall
Philadelphia, Pennsylvania

A comprehensive environmental graphics and wayfinding sign program is essential to any large facility, and the new Jon M. Huntsman Hall at the University of Pennsylvania's Wharton School of Business in Philadelphia, designed by Kohn Pedersen Fox Associates as architect with Poulin + Morris as environmental graphic designer, demonstrates how satisfying the result can be. Encompassing 324,000 square feet that feature 48 classrooms, 57 group study rooms, 500-seat forum and 300-seat auditorium, Huntsman Hall is more than Wharton's biggest building. It's the focus of Wharton's culture, exemplifying the learning, community, teamwork and innovation sustaining the school since 1881. Consequently, Poulin + Morris worked closely with the architect and the school to produce award-winning building identification, directional, informational, office and classroom identification and regulatory signs. Since Huntsman Hall was financed entirely by philanthropic gifts, Poulin + Morris also developed a donor recognition program whose central component is a 40-foot wall of 306 glass panels in the main entrance corridor. Each panel consists of a decorative back pane and typographic front pane. The delicate linework patterns on back panes, refined by hand and translated into forms that are sandblasted into glass, are derived from antique Wedgwood transferware patterns originally commissioned for the University and formerly applied to china for donor gifts. By contrast, front panes remain blank until they are etched with donors' names and infilled with white-gold leaf. This thoughtful arrangement ensures that the wall always appears complete, even before new donor names arrive.

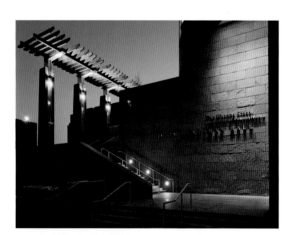

Right: Donor recognition sign

Far right: Donor recognition wall

Below: Detail of donor recognition wall

Opposite below, clockwise from upper left: Building identification, room identification, detail of building identification, directional sign

Photography: Jeffrey Totaro

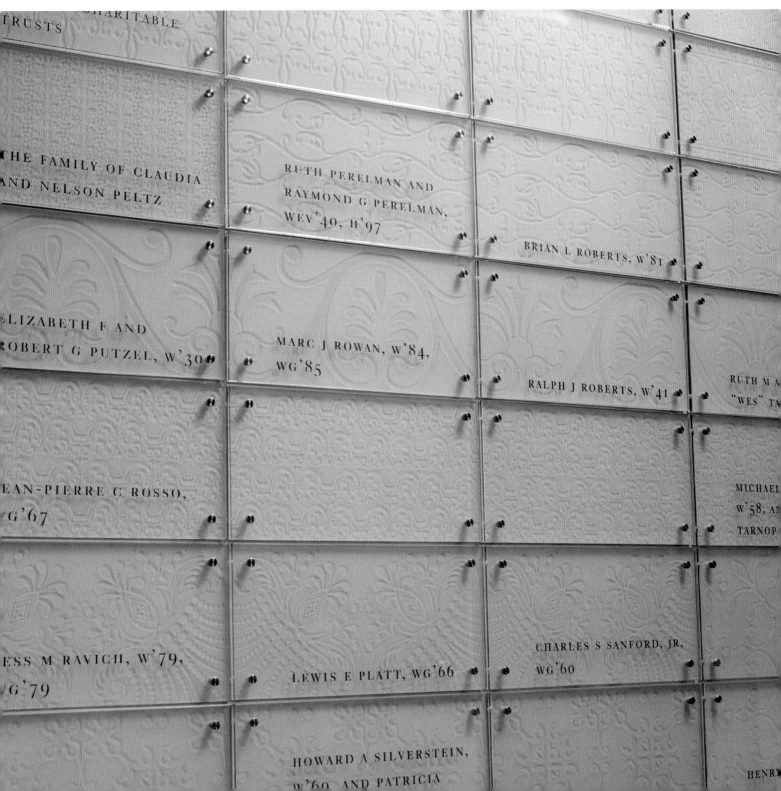

TRUSTS   CHARITABLE

THE FAMILY OF CLAUDIA
AND NELSON PELTZ

RUTH PERELMAN AND
RAYMOND G PERELMAN,
WEV'40, H'97

BRIAN L ROBERTS, W'81

ELIZABETH F AND
ROBERT G PUTZEL, W'30

MARC J ROWAN, W'84,
WG'85

RALPH J ROBERTS, W'41

RUTH M A
"WES" TA

EAN-PIERRE C ROSSO,
G'67

MICHAEL
W'58, AN
TARNOP

ESS M RAVICH, W'79,
G'79

LEWIS E PLATT, WG'66

CHARLES S SANFORD, JR,
WG'60

HOWARD A SILVERSTEIN,
W'60 AND PATRICIA

HENRY

Poulin + Morris Inc.

Syracuse University
S. I. Newhouse School of Public Communications
Syracuse, New York

Space that encourages collaboration among students and faculty is one of the distinguishing features of the new, 74,000-square-foot addition to Syracuse University's 66,000-square-foot S. I. Newhouse School of Public Communications, one of America's leading schools of mass communication. The new facility, designed by Polshek Partnership Architects as architect with Poulin + Morris as environmental graphic designer, focuses on interdisciplinary study inside a glass-wrapped structure housing classrooms, conference center, auditorium, high-tech media laboratories, editing suites, research centers, student lounges, dining area and offices. It also showcases new forms of media. In developing an environmental graphics and donor recognition program to link the various areas of the Newhouse complex, Poulin + Morris chose to infuse the new building with diverse media converging in the digital world. One result is the unique donor recognition wall in the entrance lobby, where 100-plus wall-mounted horizontal LED digital panels simulate news zippers in displaying donors' names and personal messages. Another is a large-scale typographic wall mural occupying the three-story atrium, identifying "NEWHOUSE" and its programs with CMYK-colored halftone dots that celebrate traditional and non-traditional forms of communications in the new digital era.

The final component is a large-scale typographic wall mural celebrating the importance of the First Amendment's freedom of speech, the press, and its integral relationship to the mission of the S. I. Newhouse School of Public Communications. Wherever you look, the visual solutions function as meaningful symbols—both established and emerging—of mass communication.

Left: Building exterior

Lower left: Detail of LED digital donor recognition wall

Bottom left: First Amendment recognition wall

Bottom right: Donor recognition wall

Opposite: Atrium wall mural

Photography: Jeffrey Totaro

Poulin + Morris Inc.

Pennsylvania State University
Smeal College of Business
State College, Pennsylvania

It's not uncommon for Pennsylvania State University to establish commanding positions in academic fields it enters through diligent, long-term investment in teaching, research and public service. Consider the new, four-story, 210,000-square-foot Smeal College of Business, designed by Robert A.M. Stern Architects as architect and Poulin + Morris as environmental graphic designer, at the State College campus. The state-of-the-art facility, offering classrooms, lecture halls, research and teaching laboratories, conference and meeting rooms, along with a four-story atrium, 400-seat auditorium, and "Blue Chip" café, caps the College's development from a 1953 founding to today's

world-class institution. Poulin + Morris developed a comprehensive environmental graphics, donor recognition and wayfinding sign program to complement the new building. Along with such basic components as building, departmental, classroom and office identification, directional, wayfinding and informational signs, thematic graphic murals for the café's servery, and regulatory signs, the project features an extensive donor recognition program. For the donor recognition wall, donors' names are incised on the fronts of individual glass panels against an iconographic background, derived from textural line patterns used in stock certificates, bonds and international currency, that

is sandblasted on the backs. The program aptly celebrates the support of donors—and the institution that educated them.

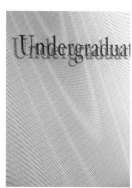

Poulin + Morris Inc.

Lycée Français de New York
New York, New York

Founded in 1935, the Lycée Français de New York is a prestigious private school that has flourished despite being spread over six landmark townhouses in Manhattan's Upper East Side. Now, the school occupies a splendid new, five-story, 163,000-square-foot building, designed by Polshek Partnership Architects as architect and Poulin + Morris as environmental graphic designer (as well as developer of design criteria and standards for all donor recognition requirements), that not only unites everyone under one roof, it frees them from landmark building restrictions. The design of the environmental graphics, donor recognition and wayfinding sign program for its classrooms, science and art centers, gymnasiums, cafeteria, offices and outdoor recreation space affords a fascinating look at cultural diversity. While 80 percent of K-12 instruction is in French, the 1,000 students are 40 percent French, 40 percent American and 20 percent from other countries. Consequently, the sign program must transcend language, nationality and age boundaries. The result, based on simple geometry and bold color coding, succeeds with a look that reinforces the Lycée's stunning architecture. Among its unique features are the large elliptical stainless steel panels applied with the school's crest and installed at each main entrance, room identification panels created with placeholders for corresponding class attendance and room schedule inserts, and the 10-foot-high granite base wall, sandblasted with a horizontal pattern comprising the names of nearly 500 international innovators. The base wall encircles the entire building and leaves no doubt what the Lycée Français de New York expects of its graduates.

Above left: Building entrance with school crest

Far left: Room identification with class attendance and room schedule inserts

Left: Building exterior

Below: Granite base sandblasted with names of international innovators

Photography: Jeffrey Totaro

224

Roll • Barresi & Associates

Roll • Barresi & Associates

Harvard Business School
Exterior and Interior Sign Program
Cambridge, Massachusetts

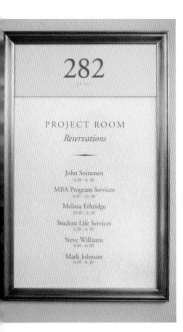

Left: Building identification

Far left: Room identification

Right: Building directory

Below right: Carved lettering

Clockwise from lower left: Campus identification, Baker Library façade, freestanding directional sign, freestanding library section identification

Photography: Roll, Barresi & Associates and Greg Premru

While Harvard Business School, the institution that introduced the case method in 1925, remains a pacesetter in business education, the 33 buildings on its 40-acre Cambridge campus honor the Georgian-style architecture it embraced after leaving Harvard Yard in 1927. The campus is meticulously maintained. For over a decade and through numerous building and landscape projects, for example, Roll, Barresi & Associates has been working with the school to produce a comprehensive system of exterior campus and interior building signage. This includes campus identification signs, donor recognitions, memorials to alumni and faculty, and most recently, pedestrian campus orientation maps. Typical program elements enhance two recent projects developed with Robert A.M. Stern Architects, the new Spangler Student Center and the renovation and addition to historic Baker Library. The signs reflect and reinforce the buildings' distinctive architecture while serving as a standard for existing and future buildings. Traditional materials and higher-grade finishes consistent with the architecture serve public "front of house" signs, and simpler profiles and neutral colors furnish private "back of house" signs, with wayfinding in historically sensitive areas employing freestanding elements to gain flexibility and avoid affixing signs where none were originally intended--one of many such details appreciated at Harvard.

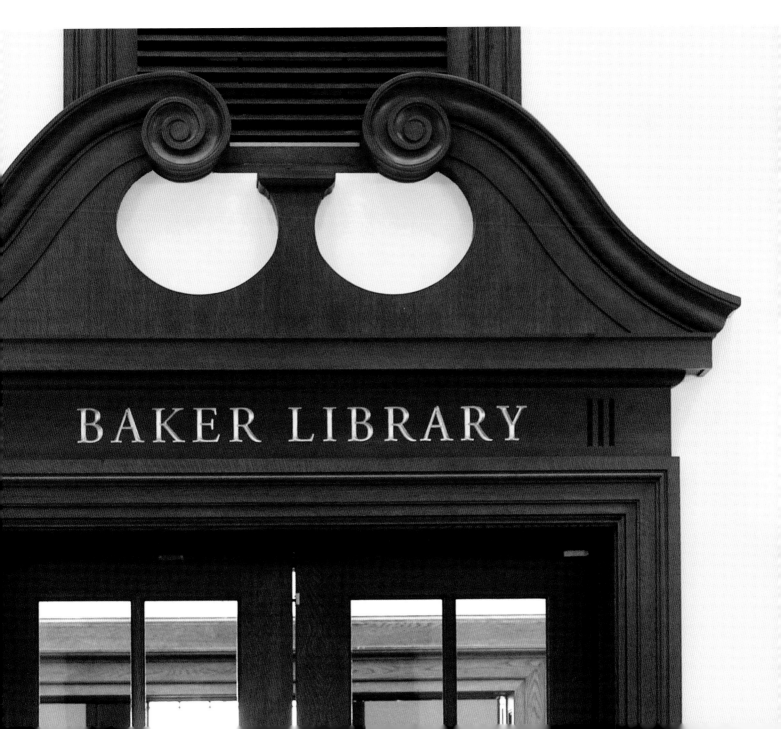

Roll • Barresi & Associates

Kenyon College
Athletic Center
Sign and Graphics Program
Gambier, Ohio

Proclaiming that sports and recreation play important roles in academic life, Kenyon College, one of the nation's leading liberal arts colleges, recently completed a superb new Athletic Center on its 1,000-acre campus in Gambier. Ohio. The 263,000-square-foot space, designed by Gund Partnership, houses all team and intramural sports facilities, along with extensive provisions for recreation and fitness, under an arching structure of steel and glass. The challenge for its environmental graphics and signage program, designed by Roll, Barresi & Associates, was twofold. First, the college sought a compelling display of graphics and information to convey the story of its athletics in a form equal to the building's scale and drama. In addition, people needed a comprehensive signage and wayfinding program, integrated and responsive to the architecture and finishes, to direct them to their destinations. The program has delivered on both counts. The athletics display wall features a digitally printed wallcovering of historic and contemporary images combined with a system of glass panels holding digital prints on clear film, interchangeable prints that display individual and team awards. The sign program, comprising room identification signs, wayfinding and donor recognition in engraved stainless steel, mirrors the building's finishes. They're a win-win for Kenyon.

Roll • Barresi & Associates

Illinois Wesleyan University
Ames Library
Sign and Graphics Program
Normal, Illinois

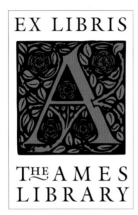

"We stand in a position of incalculable responsibility to the great wave of population overspreading the valley of the Mississippi…" is the dramatic opening stanza to a quotation carved into the Founders' Gate at the west entrance to Illinois Wesleyan University, in Normal, Illinois. The lettering may be time-worn, but its call to destiny survives as a stenciled frieze in the central rotunda of the new, five-level, 103,000-square-foot Ames Library, designed by Shepley Bulfinch Richardson & Abbott, at the heart of the 80-acre campus. High-minded thinking is not unusual at Illinois Wesleyan, a respected liberal arts university established by civic and Methodist Church leaders in 1850. The signage and architectural graphics program for the library, developed by Roll, Barresi & Associates, simultaneously celebrates its design and reflects its importance in campus life. Accordingly, the Arts & Crafts-inspired decorative border that encircles the rotunda and adorns major public spaces is carried through the sign program to provide a unifying theme and integrate the wayfinding and signage with the building's architecture. A bookplate motif was also developed for the library's use on letterheads, bookmarks and other printed materials, giving the library a distinctive image and identity worthy of this serious-minded school.

Top left: Bookplate

Below left: Rotunda

Bottom left: Circulation desk identification sign

Below right: Craftsman applying decorative border in rotunda

Opposite: Main entrance with hand-carved lettering in limestone

Photography: Peter Mauss

Roll • Barresi & Associates

Bennington College
Campus Sign and Wayfinding Program
Bennington, Vermont

Sited on a rolling 470-acre former estate in the southern Vermont town of Bennington amid woodlands, wetlands, views of the Green Mountains and buildings ranging from original barns and outbuildings to recently completed student residences designed by Kyu Sung Woo, Bennington College represents a bucolic academic community for 759 undergraduate and graduate students. The school's campus and distinguished programs in the visual and performing arts inspired Roll, Barresi & Associates in designing a campus sign and wayfinding program that would resonate with the landscape and reflect the academic focus on the arts. Introducing a signage system based on Cor Ten® steel, a material that rusts over time and is often used for outdoor sculpture, the design team developed simple, slab shapes that seemingly emerge from the landscape to support sign messages in matte stainless steel.

However, the program offers notable exceptions to this distinctly organic imagery—in the deliberately bright and colorful regulatory signs and temporary signs printed on magnetic sheeting to adhere to the Cor Ten® slabs. Seen on the grounds of the school, the complete sign program, comprising identification, direction, information and regulatory signing, looks as much at home as the natural and man-made objects it complements.

Top: Main campus identification sign

Above right: Building identification with magnetic event sign

Above far right: Building identification sign

Right: Parking identification sign

Far right: Building lettering

Photography: Roll, Barresi & Associates

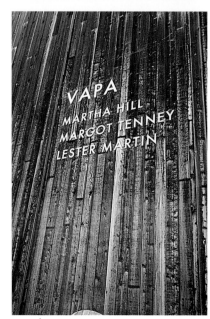

232

Selbert Perkins Design

Selbert Perkins Design

Columbia University
Gary C. Comer Geochemistry Building/
Lamont-Dougherty Earth Observatory
Palisades, New York

With concern rising about humanity's environmental impact on the earth, scientists at Columbia University who study of the role of chemical substances in air, oceans, groundwater, biological remains, sediment and rock have come out of the kitchen to occupy the new, two-story, 67,000-square-foot Gary C. Comer Geochemistry Building at the Lamont-Doherty Earth Observatory, in Palisades, New York. Lamont's geochemists began working in the kitchen of the Observatory's original building in the 1950s, and subsequently spread across the Lamont campus. Now, the state-of-the-art facility, designed by Payette Associates as architect with Selbert Perkins Design as environmental graphics designer and exhibition designer, provides over 70 offices and 30 laboratories in one location for scientists, students and support staff. Named for the late Gary C. Comer, founder of the Lands' End apparel company and a major donor to the project, the modern, metal-and-glass structure projects a bold image highlighted by the main identity sign and exhibits telling the story of Comer and the science of geochemistry, blended seamlessly into the space. The graphics and exhibition elements relate directly to the architecture and the science, incorporating stainless steel, granite, wood, glass and large-scale imagery in timeless, modern forms to attract, educate and inspire both occupants and visitors.

Left: Main identity sign

Below: Main entrance in evening view

Opposite below: Bust of Gary C. Comer and accompanying exhibit

Photography: Peter Vanderwarker, Jared Zagha

Selbert Perkins Design

Massachusetts Institute of Technology
Cecil and Ida Green Center for Physics
Cambridge, Massachusetts

Most physicists probably don't contemplate the roofs over their heads, but a new facility on the 168-acre campus of Massachusetts Institute of Technology, in Cambridge, Massachusetts, has captured their attention. The Cecil and Ida Green Center for Physics, the cornerstone of a major building and renovation program known as PDSI, designed by Payette Associates as architect and Selbert Perkins Design as environmental graphics designer, gives MIT's Department of Physics a long-sought place of its own. Even so, the Center is a complex amalgam of old and new construction, incorporating the fourth floor of Building 6, the first, second, third and fourth floors of 6C (a new "infill" structure replacing 6A), and the third floors of Buildings 4, 6 and 8 within the "Main Group," MIT's historic and interconnected Bosworth Buildings, designed by William Welles Bosworth and completed around 1916. The Center's environmental graphics combine bluestone-based signs, which form a continuous datum line that orients and defines circulation, room identity and donor recognition, with dynamic LED monitors and floor murals by artist Sol Lewitt to identify, unify and link classrooms, research laboratories, common areas and circulation corridors. As a result, MIT's physicists will have no trouble finding their way "home."

Above: Donor recognition display

Bottom left and right: Room identification signs

Opposite: Atrium in Building 6C with Sol Lewitt floor murals

Photography: Peter Vanderwarker, Jared Zagha

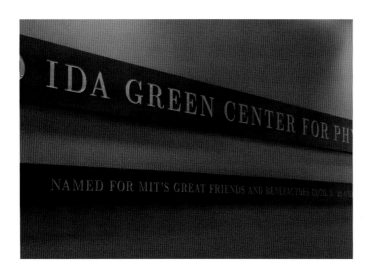

Selbert Perkins Design

University of Southern California
USC Graphic Standards
Los Angeles, California

Developing a unified graphic standard for a university campus that preserves the individual identities of colleges, programs and sports teams is a formidable task when the school is the University of Southern California, an institution dating back to 1880, and its campus is University Park, a 226-acre expanse in the heart of Los Angeles' Downtown Arts and Education Corridor where the bulk of its 33,500 undergraduate and graduate students and 11,700 faculty members and staff reside. So when Selbert Perkins Design was asked to prepare the master plan, design and implementation of USC's graphic standards, it created a solution that links the school's brand—its logo, color and typography—with each sub-brand's name and logo. The system affords USC branding flexibility while providing a consistent foundation for all visual communications. Its success as an award-winning system in use for over a decade can be witnessed even now as it expands and evolves to meet new and unprecedented needs and applications. A simple kit-of-parts solution,

it functions as "branded furniture" for the campus that is easy to maintain and update using stainless steel and aluminum components and a branded color system, keeping USC in touch with its past, present and future.

Left: Campus directional signs

Far left: Outdoor banners for building identification

Below left: Interior building identification signage

Below right: Interior conference room with banners

Photography: Anton Grassl

Selbert Perkins Design

Salem State College
Communications Master Plan and Graphic Standards
Salem, Massachusetts

Over the last 150 years, Salem State College, in Salem, Massachusetts, has evolved from Salem Normal School, a teacher's college founded in 1854, into its current form as a multi-purpose institution of higher education, serving some 10,000 students in graduate and undergraduate programs on the 108-acre campus that has been its home since the 1890s. The school has thrived because it closely monitors what the public wants to know and maintains close contact with its constituency, which includes the state government that approves its budgets. Thus, when it retained Selbert Perkins Design to create a unified graphic standard for its print, Web pages, environmental design and merchandise, it enlisted local, state and institutional groups to help define the brand, key images and messages. The award-winning graphic standard is credited with establishing an appealing public image that is seen and liked by students, faculty, staff, alumni and other friends and support-ers, as well as the public at large. A typical example of the standard's effectiveness is the campus signage, which is shaped like a ship's sail, reflecting the school's core brand image. It's just one reason why Salem State has referred to Selbert Perkins Design as an "invaluable partner."

Left: Examples of outdoor sig-nage on the Salem State campus
Photography: Anton Grassl

Design with light.™

Resources*

Alvernia University, Campus Commons
Design Firm: Derck & Edson Associates
Furniture: DuMor
Lighting: AAL
General Contractors: Associated Contractors
Lighting Consultants: Consolidated Engineers

Alvord Unified School District, Innovative Learning Center
Design Firm: HMC Architects
Furniture: Community Playthings, Haworth, KI
Carpets & Flooring: Azrock, Daltile, Interceramic, Mohawk
Fabrics: Pallas Textiles
Lighting: Bega, Daybrite, Gammalux, Lightolier, Louis Poulsen, Prudential
Ceilings: Armstrong
Wallcoverings and Paint: Dunn Edwards, Koroseal
General Contractors: Neff Construction, Inc.

Bard College at Simon's Rock, Daniel Arts Center
Design Firm: Ann Beha Architects
Furniture: American Seating
Carpets & Flooring: Atlas, Daltile, Robbins Bio Channel, Rosco Tiles
Lighting: Cole, HessAmerica, Halophane, Kurt Versen, Lightolier, Lithonia
Ceilings: GWB, Tectum
General Contractors: Mullaney Corporation
Lighting Consultants: Ripman Associates

Belmont University, Bill and Carole Troutt Theater
Design Firm: Earl Swensson Associates, Inc. (ESa)
Furniture: Track Seating
Carpets & Flooring: Crossville, Monterey, Nora Rubber
Lighting: Davis/Muller Lighting
Ceilings: Armstrong
Wallcoverings and Paint: Porter Paint
Window Treatments: MechoShade
General Contractors: American Constructors, Inc.

Belmont University, Gordon E. Inman Center, College of Health Sciences & Nursing
Design Firm: Earl Swensson Associates, Inc. (ESa)
Carpets & Flooring: Daltile, Lees, Monterey
Wallcoverings and Paint: Evans & Brown, Eykon, Maharam, MDC, National Wallcover, Porter Paint

Belmont University, Residence Hall
Design Firm: Earl Swensson Associates, Inc. (ESa)
Carpets & Flooring: Estrie Vinyl Tile, Forbo, Marmoleum, Shaw Contract
Lighting: Hadco, Stenberg
Ceilings: USG

Wallcoverings and Paint: Construction Specialties, Porter Paint
Window Treatments: Caco
General Contractors: R.C. Matthews Contractor

Berkeley High School Student Union and Recreation Center
Design Firm: ELS Architecture and Urban Design
Furniture: Agati, Warden
Carpets & Flooring: Connor, Daltile, Mohawk
Lighting: I.L.C., Novitus
Ceilings: Armstrong
Wallcoverings and Paint: USG
Window Treatments: Kawneer, MechoShade, PPG
General Contractors: Arntz Construction
Lighting Consultants: Silverman & Light

Birmingham Southern College Urban Environmental Park
Design Firm: Derck & Edson Associates
Lighting: AAL
General Contractors: Johnson Kreis Construction
Lighting Consultants: CRS Engineering Inc.

Bloomsburg University of Pennsylvania, Academic Quadrangle
Design Firm: Derck & Edson Associates
Furniture: Phoenician by Ironsmith, Wabash Valley Mnfg
Lighting: Gardco, Hadco, Hydrel, Intense, Solavanti
General Contractors: Don E. Bower, Inc.
Lighting Consultants: Consolidated Engineers

Boston University, School of Hospitality Administration
Design Firm: Elkus Manfredi Architects
Furniture: Cappellini, Halcon, KI, Knoll, Tuohy
Carpets & Flooring: Axminster, Constantine, Endura, Parterre Vinyl Flooring, Thai Dynasty Carpets
Fabrics: Glant, Knoll, Maharam
Lighting: Artemide, Corelite, Edison Price, Flos, Gotham, Ledalite, Litecontrol, Lithonia
Ceilings: Armstrong, Ecophon, GWB
Wallcoverings and Paint: Benjamin Moore, Knoll, Wolf-Gordon
Window Treatments: Henia Eizenberg, Levolor, Maharam Kvadrat
General Contractors: Suffolk Construction
Lighting Consultants: Lam Partners

Brentwood Academy, Fine Arts Center
Design Firm: Earl Swensson Associates, Inc. (ESa)
Furniture: HON, Merck and Hill, Oxford English Gardens, Wenger
Carpets & Flooring: American Olean, Bomanite, Mannington, NeoShok, Patene Artectura, Shaw Contract

Ceilings: Armstrong
Wallcoverings and Paint: Benjamin Moore, Duroplex, Triarch Industries
Window Treatments: MechoShade
General Contractors: American Constructors, Inc.

Bridgewater State College, Crimson Hall
Design Firm: DiMella Shaffer
Furniture: Adden, Allermuir, Davis, KI
Carpets & Flooring: Armstrong, Milliken, Mirage Tile, Shaw
Fabrics: Carnegie, Maharam, Momentum, Pollack
Lighting: Axis, Daybrite, Day-O-Lite, Omega, Teron
Ceilings: Armstrong, Ecophon
Wallcoverings and Paint: ICI Paint
Window Treatments: Castec, Phifer
General Contractors: Walsh Brothers, Inc.
Lighting Consultants: Kaplan Gehring McCarroll Architectural Lighting

California State University, Dominguez Hills, Loker Student Union
Design Firm: Cannon Design
Furniture: Academia, Allermuir, Brayton, Cassina, EMU, Fritz Hansen, GF Office, Gordon International, Janus et Cie, Johanson, Kartell, Magis, Metro, Palmer Snyder, Steelmobile, Swedese
Carpets & Flooring: Azrock, Collins & Aikman, Daltile, Johnsonite, Lithochrome Chemstain, LM Scofield
Ceilings: Armstrong
Wallcoverings and Paint: Abet Laminate, Formica, Frazee, Knoll, Maharam, Modernfold, Nevamar, Pionite, 3Form, Varia, Vertu
General Contractors: S.J. Amoroso

Cape Cod Community College, Lyndon P. Lorusso Applied Technology Building
Design Firm: DiMella Shaffer
Carpets & Flooring: Cermica Fioranese Tile, Interface
Lighting: Finelite
Ceilings: Ecophon
Wallcoverings and Paint: Benjamin Moore
Window Treatments: MechoShade
General Contractors: A.P. Whitaker & Sons
Lighting Consultants: Sylvan R. Shemitz Associates

Case Western Reserve University, Mandel Center for Nonprofit Organizations
Design Firm: Kallmann McKinnell & Wood Architects, Inc.
Furniture: Knoll
Carpets & Flooring: Bentley, Floor Gres
Fabrics: Knoll
Lighting: Axis, Fontana Arte
Ceilings: Armstrong

If Walls Could Talk

Walls and ceilings would request Novawall® stretch fabric coverings, the system with sustainable LEED credit attributes.

Novawall® is the industry leader for stretch fabrics used in sustainable interior design. Novawall® uses EcoTRACK, the first PVC-free extrusion process in the industry, and features recycled content core materials as well as fabrics made with renewable/recyclable content.

With Ecogear, Novawall®'s contributions calculator, we'll analyze LEED credit contributions and prepare the paperwork for you, which makes Novawall® the ecologically responsible choice for your project, and the right business choice for you.

NOVAWALL SYSTEMS, INC.

The Standard for Fabric Wall and Ceiling Systems

MEMBER

800.695.6682

sales@novawall.com

www.novawall.com

Wallcoverings and Paint: Benjamin Moore, Decoustics, Guilford of Maine
Window Treatments: MechoShade
General Contractors: A.M. Higley
Lighting Consultants: Collaborative Lighting

Cazenovia College, Art & Design Building
Design Firm: HOLT Architects, P.C.
Furniture: Design Option, KI, Mayline, Patrician
Carpets & Flooring: Armstrong, Daltile, J&J, Johnsonite, Wassau
Fabrics: Dallas, Maharam
Lighting: Columbia, Kenall, Kim, Liana, Litecontrol, Louis Poulsen, Lucifer, Prescolite, Tivoli, Vista
Ceilings: Armstrong
Wallcoverings and Paint: Devoe
Window Treatments: Bali
General Contractors: Northeast Construction Services

Central Middle School
Design Firm: Perkins+Will, design architect; CSO Architects, Inc., architect of record
Furniture: Brodart, V/S America, Wenger
Carpets & Flooring: American Olean, Crossville, Mannington, Terrazzo
Ceilings: USG
Wallcoverings and Paint: Architectural Components Group, Benjamin Moore, Daltile
Window Treatments: Hunter Douglas
General Contractors: Dunlap Construction
Lighting Consultants: L'Acquis Consulting Engineers

Colgate University, Glendening Boathouse
Design Firm: HOLT Architects, P.C.
Carpets & Flooring: Daltile, J&J, Mannington
Lighting: Columbia, Kenall, Louis Poulsen, Luminus, Luraline, Prescolite, Visa
Ceilings: Armstrong
Wallcoverings and Paint: ICI Paint
General Contractors: Whelen & Curry

Cragmont Elementary School
Design Firm: ELS Architecture and Urban Design
Furniture: YAG Manufacturing
Carpets & Flooring: Armstrong, Daltile, Mohawk, Oregon Lumber Co.
Lighting: Architectural Area Lighting, Bega, Litecontrol, Louis Poulsen
Ceilings: Armstrong
Wallcoverings and Paint: Dunn Edwards
Window Treatments: U.S. Aluminum, Viacon
General Contractors: West Bay Builders
Lighting Consultants: Silverman & Light

Emerson College, The Paramount Center
Design Firm: Elkus Manfredi Architects
Furniture: Falvey Finishing, Irwin, John Savoy and Sons
Carpets & Flooring: Axminster, Environglass Terrazzo, Tandus Monterey
Fabrics: KM, Momentum, Thermotex

Lighting: Crenshaw, Intense Lighting, Lithonia, LSI, Mark Lighting, Zumtobel Staff
Ceilings: Armstrong, Ecophon
Wallcoverings and Paint: Benjamin Moore
Window Treatments: Draper, MechoShade
General Contractors: Bond Brothers Incorporated
Lighting Consultants: Cline, Bettridge, Bernstein Lighting Design Inc.

Fairmont State University, Falcon Center
Design Firm: VOA Associates Incorporated
Furniture: All Seating, Allsteel, David Edward
Carpets & Flooring: Armstrong, Beynon Sports Surfaces, Masland
Lighting: Allsteel
Wallcoverings and Paint: American Olean, Benjamin Moore

First Presbyterian Church of Berkeley, Christian Education Center
Design Firm: ELS Architecture and Urban Design
Carpets & Flooring: Durkan, Karastan
Fabrics: Guilford of Maine
Ceilings: Rulon
Wallcoverings and Paint: Benjamin Moore, Sherwin-Williams
Window Treatments: MechoShade
General Contractors: Overaa Construction
Lighting Consultants: Auerbach + Glasnow

Grand Theatre Center for the Arts
Design Firm: ELS Architecture and Urban Design
Carpets & Flooring: Daltile, Floric Polytech, Masland
Fabrics: JB Martin, Maharam
Wallcoverings and Paint: Frazee, Kelly Moore, Rosco
Window Treatments: MechoShade
General Contractors: McFadden Construction Inc.

Harvard University, Graduate Commons
Design Firm: Elkus Manfredi Architects
Furniture: Adden Furniture, Bernhardt, Gunlocke, Herman Miller, Integra
Carpets & Flooring: Atmosphere, Corbo Marmoleum, Johnsonite, Mohawk, Plyboo, Shaw, Tuva
Fabrics: ArcCom
Lighting: Bega, Delray, Edison Price, Kim Lighting, Leucos, Mark Lighting, Oxygen, Shaper, Tre Ci Luce
Ceilings: Ecophon, GWB, USG
Wallcoverings and Paint: Dutch Boy
Window Treatments: Draper, MechoShade
General Contractors: John Moriarty & Associates, Inc.
Lighting Consultants: Sladen Feinstein

Hector P. Garcia Middle School
Design Firm: Perkins+Will
Furniture: Biofit Engineered Products, Community, HON, Royal Seating, TASCO
Carpets & Flooring: Armstrong, Bentley Prince Street, Interface
Lighting: Lightolier

Ceilings: Armstrong
Wallcoverings and Paint: ICI Paint
Window Treatments: Levolor, MechoShade
General Contractors: Satterfield & Pontikes Construction
Lighting Consultants: Perkins+Will, Basharkhah Engineering

Johnson County Community College, Regnier Center for Business and Technology
Design Firm: Gould Evans
Furniture: Brayton, Davis, Herman Miller, Jofco, Keilhauer, Knoll, Teknion
Carpets & Flooring: Atlas, Bentley Prince Street, Lees, Wausau Tile
Fabrics: Architex, DesignTex, Maharam
Lighting: Derek Porter Studio, LAM Partners
Ceilings: Armstrong, Ecophon
Wallcoverings and Paint: Desco, ICI Paints
Window Treatments: Allied Glass Experts, LLC
General Contractors: JE Dunn Construction Co.
Lighting Consultants: Derek Porter Studio, LAM Partners, Inc.

Lafayette College, David Bishop Skillman Library Renovation and Expansion
Design Firm: Ann Beha Architects
Carpets & Flooring: American Olean, Ardex Topping, Bloomsburg, Bolyu, Expanko
Ceilings: Armstrong, Rulon, Sound Concepts Canada
Window Treatments: MechoShade
General Contractors: Turner Construction Company

Los Angeles County High School for the Arts
Design Firm: HMC Architects
Carpets & Flooring: Ergon Engineered Stone, Monterey, Plyboo
Lighting: ALights, Designplan, Engineered Lighting Products, Ledalite, Linear, Martin, Prudential, TIR
Ceilings: Armstrong
Wallcoverings and Paint: Dunn Edwards, Ergon Engineered Stone, Illbruck
Window Treatments: Roll Shades

Los Angeles Unified School District, High School for the Visual and Performing Arts
Design Firm: HMC Architects/coop Himmelb(1)au
Carpets & Flooring: Interface
Fabrics: Rose Brand
Lighting: Prudential
Ceilings: USG
Wallcoverings and Paint: Dunn Edwards
Window Treatments: Skyco Shading Systems
General Contractors: PCL

Millennium Park, Exelon Pavilions
Design Firm: Hammond Beeby Rupert Ainge Architects, Inc.
Carpets & Flooring: Patcraft
Lighting: Compact Fluorescent, Cooper Lighting
Ceilings: USG
Wallcoverings and Paint: Sherwin-Williams

architect: Steven Holl   photography: Andy Ryan

EXPERIENCE BARTCO LIGHTING.

CUSTOM FIXTURE DESIGN. SPECIFICATION ASSISTANCE. EXCEPTIONAL LEAD TIMES.

retail . commercial . institutional . hospitality . residential

bartco LIGHTING
leading the way and lighting it.™

manufacturers of quality lighting products   tel **714.230.3200** / fax 714.230.3222 / bartcoLIGHTING.com

Window Treatments: Wausau
General Contractors: Walsh Construction Corp. of Illinois
Lighting Consultants: Hammond Beeby Rupert Ainge Architects, Inc.

North Shore Community College, Berry Academic Building
Design Firm: Dimella Shaffer
Carpets & Flooring: Shaw
Ceilings: Armstrong
Wallcoverings and Paint: Beldin Tile, Benjamin Moore
General Contractors: Congress Construction Company
Lighting Consultants: Sylvan R. Shemitz Associates

The Ohio State University, South Campus Gateway
Design Firm: Elkus Manfredi Architects
Carpets & Flooring: Monterey, To Market
Lighting: Color Kinetics, Lightolier, Source Four
Ceilings: Ceilings Plus, Ecophon
Wallcoverings and Paint: Lumicor, Panelite, Pittsburgh Paints
General Contractors: Turner Construction Company
Lighting Consultants: Kaplan Gehring McCarroll Architectural Lighting

Plymouth State University, Langdon Woods Residence Hall
Design Firm: Cannon Design
Furniture: Aceray, Brayton, Bretford, Davis, DCI, Keilhauer, KI, Teknion
Carpets & Flooring: Armstrong, Azrock, Floor Gres, Johnsonite, PacifiCrest
Lighting: Cooper, Litecontrol
Ceilings: Armstrong
Wallcoverings and Paint: Alkemi, Avonite, FSC, Nevamar, Sherwin-Williams, USG, Wilsonart
Window Treatments: MechoShade, Solarban
General Contractors: Engelberth Construction

Princeton University, Clio Hall, Additions and Renovations
Design Firm: Hammond Beeby Rupert Ainge Architects, Inc.
Furniture: Geiger, Herman Miller, Knoll
Carpets & Flooring: Tarkett
Fabrics: Herman Miller, Knoll
Lighting: Focal Point, New Metal Crafts
Ceilings: USG
Wallcoverings and Paint: Benjamin Moore, MAB Paint
Window Treatments: Levolor
General Contractors: Barr & Barr, Inc.
Lighting Consultants: Schuler and Shook, Inc.

Reading Area Community College, Miller Center for the Arts
Design Firm: Kallmann McKinnell & Wood Architects, Inc.

Carpets & Flooring: Constantine Commercial
Lighting: Alkco
Ceilings: Armstrong
Wallcoverings and Paint: Benjamin Moore, Decoustics, Duron
General Contractors: Hayes Construction
Lighting Consultants: Berg Howland Associates

Southern Methodist University, Meadows Museum
Design Firm: Hammond Beeby Rupert Ainge Architects, Inc.
General Contractors: Austin Commercial
Lighting Consultants: Claude Eagle

South Junion High School
Design Firm: Gould Evans
Furniture: Palmer Hamilton
Carpets & Flooring: J&J Commercial, Robbins Hardwood Floors
Lighting: Architectural Area Lighting, Bruck, Focal Point, Hubbell Lighting, Infinity Lighting, Kim Lighting, Litecontrol, Martin Lighting, WattStopper
Ceilings: Celotex, Hunter Douglas
Wallcoverings and Paint: Sherwin-Williams
Window Treatments: Bali Contract
General Contractors: Ferrell Construction
Lighting Consultants: Mercer-Zimmerman, Inc., Derek Porter Studio

State University of New York, Upstate Medical Center, Setner Academic Building
Design Firm: HOLT Architects, P.C.
Carpets & Flooring: Armstrong, Crossville, J&J
Fabrics: Carnegie Xorel, Strie
Lighting: Beta Cako, Daybrite
Ceilings: Armstrong, Illbruck
Wallcoverings and Paint: Kinetics, RPG, Sherwin-Williams
General Contractors: Murnane Building Contractors
Lighting Consultants: Naomi Miller

Susquehanna University, West Village
Design Firm: Derck & Edson Associates
Furniture: DuMor
Lighting: Hapco, Lithonia
General Contractors: R.S. Mowery & Sons, Inc.

Texas Tech University Health Sciences Center, El Paso, Paul L. Foster School of Medicine, Medical Education Building
Design Firm: CO Architects
Carpets & Flooring: Armstrong, Dex-o-Tex, Eco Floor, Mohawk, Patcraft, Shaw
Fabrics: Maharam
Lighting: Bega, Kim, Linear, Lithonia, Metalux, Portfolio, Selux
Ceilings: Symphony, USG
Wallcoverings and Paint: QTS Panels, Sherwin-Williams, Symphony
Window Treatments: Hunter Douglas, MechoShade

General Contractors: Vaughn Construction
Lighting Consultants: Kaplan Gehring McCarroll

University of Arizona, Law Commons at James E. Rogers College of Law
Design Firm: Gould Evans
Furniture: Artifort, Harter, Steelcase
Carpets & Flooring: Interface
Fabrics: Knoll, Maharam, Momentum
Lighting: Bega, Litecontrol, Lithonia, Peerlite
Ceilings: Hunter Douglas
Wallcoverings and Paint: Sherwin-Williams
Window Treatments: MechoShade
General Contractors: Hansel Phelps
Lighting Consultants: Bridgers & Paxton

University of California, Los Angeles, Engineering V
Design Firm: CO Architects
Furniture: Steelcase
Carpets & Flooring: Armstrong, Mannington, Shaw
Fabrics: Knoll Textiles
Lighting: Bega, Portfolio, Zumtobel
Ceilings: Armstrong
Wallcoverings and Paint: Frazee Paint
Window Treatments: Levolor, MechoShade
General Contractors: Totor Saliba Corporation
Lighting Consultants: Kaplan Gehring McCarrol Lighting

University of California, Riverside, Physical Sciences Building
Design Firm: Kallmann McKinnell & Wood Architects, Inc. in association with HGA Architects & Engineering
Carpets & Flooring: Armstrong, Bentley
Ceilings: Armstrong
Wallcoverings and Paint: Benjamin Moore
Window Treatments: MechoShade
General Contractors: Pinner Construction

University of California, San Diego, Rady School of Management, Phase 1
Design Firm: HMC Architects
Carpets & Flooring: Armstrong, Atlas, Durkan, Mannington, Roppe
Fabrics: DesignTex, Formica, Lamin-Art, Nevamar, Pionite
Ceilings: Armstrong
Wallcoverings and Paint: Benjamin Moore, ICI, Maharam, Scuffmaster, Versa

University of Kansas Medical Center, Kansas Life Sciences Innovation Center
Design Firm: Cannon Design and GLPM (Treanor Architects)
Furniture: Fisher Hamilton
Carpets & Flooring: Armstrong, Karastan, Miliken, Quillen, Tarkett
Lighting: GE, Hubbell, Kenall, Lithonia, Metro, Omega
Ceilings: USG
Wallcoverings and Paint: Marcasite, Sherwin-Williams

NeoCon® World's Trade Fair
Chicago
June 15-17, 2009
neocon.com

NeoCon®
World's Trade Fair

IIDEX/NeoCon® Canada
Toronto
September 25–26, 2008
iidexneocon.com

IIDEX
NeoCon® Canada

NeoCon® East
Baltimore
October 29–30, 2008
neoconeast.com

NeoCon® East

National Exposition of Contract Furnishings
To exhibit or register to attend, visit merchandisemartproperties.com or call 800.677.6278.

Merchandise Mart
Properties, Inc.

Window Treatments: MechoShade
General Contractors: Turner Construction

University of Maine, Student Recreation and Fitness Center
Design Firm: Cannon Design
Furniture: Steelcase
Carpets & Flooring: Acer Flooring, C&A, Connor Sports Flooring, Daltile, MatsInc., Mondo America, Robbins Sports Surfaces, Tandus Group
Lighting: Lithonia, Peerless, Winona
Ceilings: Armstrong
Wallcoverings and Paint: Sherwin-Williams
General Contractors: Pizzagalli Construction Co.
Lighting Consultants: Cannon Design

University of New Hampshire, Gables Residence Hall
Design Firm: DiMella Shaffer
Carpets & Flooring: Armstrong, Collins & Aikman, Lees
Fabrics: Guilford of Maine
Lighting: Louis Poulsen, Metalux, Progress, Teron/Echelon, XTC Lighting Group
Ceilings: Armstrong, Tectum
Wallcoverings and Paint: Sherwin-Williams
Window Treatments: Hunter Douglas
General Contractors: Cutler Associates
Lighting Consultants: Berg Lighting Design

University of Notre Dame, Mendoza College of Business, Executive MBA
Design Firm: VOA Associates Incorporated
Furniture: KI
Carpets & Flooring: Flooring Resources, Mohawk
Lighting: Pinnacle Lighting
Wallcoverings and Paint: Meridienne
General Contractors: Pepper Construction

University of Pennsylvania, The Music Building Renovation and Addition
Design Firm: Ann Beha Architects
Lighting: Atlantic, Day-OlLite, Halo, Hydrel, Metalux, Surelites
Ceilings: Armstrong
General Contractors: Daniel J. Keating Company
Lighting Consultants: Ripman Lighting Consultants

University of South Florida, Marshall Student Center
Design Firm: Gould Evans
Furniture: Allermuir, Cab-Deco, Carolina, Cartwright, Davis, First Office, Global, HBF, Herman Miller, Keilhauer, Leland, MTS, Stylex, Tuohy
Carpets & Flooring: Interface, Marmoleum, Terrazzo
Fabrics: ArcCom, Knoll, Maharam, Momentum, Unika Vaev
Lighting: Louis Poulsen, Sesco
Ceilings: Armstrong, Chicago Metallic
Wallcoverings and Paint: Benjamin Moore
Window Treatments: MechoShade
General Contractors: Beck Group, Inc.

University of Washington, William H. Foege Building
Design Firm: CO Architects
Furniture: Bank + Office
Carpets & Flooring: Armstrong, Shaw
Fabrics: Knoll
Lighting: Lightolier
Ceilings: Armstrong
Wallcoverings and Paint: Sherwin-Williams
Window Treatments: Levolor, MechoShade
General Contractors: Hoffman Construction Company
Lighting Consultants: Candela

University of Wisconsin Stevens Point, Lee Sherman Dreyfus University Center, Remodeling and Addition
Design Firm: Perkins+Will
Furniture: KI, Knoll
Carpets & Flooring: Armstrong, Designweave, Fusion Commercial Carpet
Ceilings: Armstrong, Rulon
Wallcoverings and Paint: Benjamin Moore
General Contractors: Miron

University of Wisconsin, Microbial Sciences Building
Design Firm: CO Architects
Furniture: Bernhardt, Brayton, Integra, KI, Knoll, Krug, Metro, Steelcase, Taylor
Carpets & Flooring: J&J/Invision, Patcraft, Tandus, Terrazzo
Fabrics: Bernhardt, Brayton, Carnegie, DesignTex, Knoll, Momentum, Sina Pearson
Lighting: Focal Point, Litecrontrol, Lithonia, Louis Poulsen, Prescolite, Winona
Ceilings: Armstrong, Chicago Metallic
Wallcoverings and Paint: Benjamin Moore, Maharam, Wall Talkers
Window Treatments: MechoShade
General Contractors: CD Smith
Lighting Consultants: Arnold and O'Sheridan Inc.

University System of Maryland, Universities at Shady Grove, Camille Kendall Academic Center
Design Firm: Cannon Design
Carpets & Flooring: Crossville, Eco-Surfaces, Expanko, Forbo, J&J Industries, Lees, Modular, Wausau Tile
Fabrics: Corian, Maharam
Ceilings: Armstrong
Wallcoverings and Paint: Duron
General Contractors: Skanska

Wells College, Ann Wilder Stratton '46 Hall
Design Firm: HOLT Architects, P.C.
Furniture: Design Options, KI, Nevdorfer, Teknion
Carpets & Flooring: Daltile, J&J, Mannington, Waussau Tile
Fabrics: Designtex, KI, Pallas
Lighting: Alcro, Artemide, Bartco, Bodine, Columbia,

Cooper, Finelite, Liteconrol, Littlite, LSI, Neoray, Visa
Ceilings: Armstrong
Wallcoverings and Paint: Carnegie Xorel, Guilford of Maine, ICI
Window Treatments: Draper
General Contractors: LeCesse Construction
Lighting Consultants: Naomi Miller

Wesleyan University, Suzanne Lemberg Usdan University Center
Design Firm: Kallmann McKinnell & Wood Architects
Furniture: Davis
Carpets & Flooring: Forbo, Monterey
Lighting: Day-O-Lite, LAM Luminaire, Louis Poulsen, Omega Lighting, Thomas Lighting Canada
Ceilings: Armstrong
Wallcoverings and Paint: Carnegie, Benjamin Moore
Window Treatments: MechoShade
General Contractors: FIP Construction
Lighting Consultants: Berg Howland Associates

Yale University, Sterling Memorial Library, Bass Library Renovations
Design Firm: Hammond Beeby Rupert Ainge Architects, Inc.
Furniture: Dovetail, Eustis Chairs, Herman Miller, Knoll, Quarra Stone, Rud Rasmussens, Welding Works
Carpets & Flooring: Bentley Prince Street, Burlington, Daltile
Lighting: Louis Poulsen, Nessen Lighting
Ceilings: Armstrong, Baswaphon
Wallcoverings and Paint: Benjamin Moore, Motawi Tileworks, Odegard, Quartz Stone
General Contractors: Barr & Barr, Inc.
Lighting Consultants: Claude R. Engle

Post Script

How would you feel about playing in a highly competitive league where 26 percent of your team's players, including most of your seasoned veterans, are preparing to leave? The United States economy is about to find out. Some 78 million Americans born between 1946 and 1964—the notorious Baby Boomers,—are approaching the age when many will retire, lose jobs, or settle for part-time, low-pay work. Slowly but inexorably, this well-educated, outspoken and narcissistic cohort will exit the nation's businesses and institutions, making room for succeeding generations and burdening them with unsolved problems involving the economy, health care, global peacekeeping, environment and more.

To avoid that sinking feeling, America must invest vigorously in educating its young and their elders. Communities across the nation can take pride that a record 49.8 million students enrolled in public elementary and secondary schools in fall 2008. Greeting them were 3.3 million teachers, resulting in a pupil/teacher ratio of 15.3, which is lower than the ratio of 16.0 in 2000. The cost will come to $519 billion for the 2008-2009 school year for a national average expenditure of $10,418 per student. No less intensity of commitment is visible at colleges and universities, where 18.3 million students enrolled in fall 2008, an increase of some 3.0 million since fall 2000, with fall 2016 enrollment projected to reach 20.4 million.

Will education position America's workforce for the challenges of the 21st century? The Obama administration is rallying support for such strategies as strengthening early childhood learning, increasing funding for school modernization, and improving online/offline learning through wider broadband access, better curriculum and enriched professional development. Fortunately, Americans generally agree on the need for action, recognizing how much the rest of the world has gained through education—and appreciating what education means to our way of life. Despite what is now being called the Great Recession, the quest for a quality education for all Americans, supported by superior school buildings, rolls on.

Better. Faster. Greener.

You know you can rely on Grand Rapids Chair for superior quality, durability and speed. But did you know our tables and chairs offer significant environmental advantages, as well? We use certified renewable wood. Recycled steel. No-VOC paints. And a whole host of other green materials and techniques that can help you earn LEED certification. Visit our web site to learn more!

GRAND RAPIDS CHAIR COMPANY®

www.grandrapidschair.com or 1.866.4LEGS4U

Made Green in the USA

Daylighting, efficient design, color, and community leadership are among the many factors that lead to a successful and sustainable design. AIA Architects stand ready to help ensure a healthy future for us all.

The next step is **up to you.**

By providing the integrated and sustainable design solutions that modern health systems demand, an AIA Architect can help you take the next step toward sustainability and patient well-being.

Walk the Walk
Architects Leading the Sustainable Evolution^{SM}

THE AMERICAN INSTITUTE OF ARCHITECTS

Join us and together we can walk toward a more sustainable future.
Visit **www.aia.org/walkthewalk** today.

The Designer Series

Visual Reference Publications, Inc.

302 Fifth Avenue, New York, NY 10001
212.279.7000 • Fax 212.279.7014
www.visualreference.com

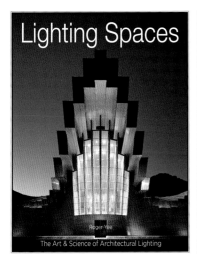

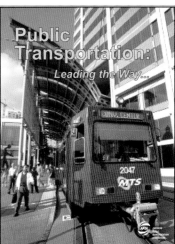

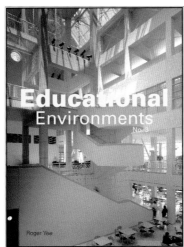

Advertiser Index

Index by Project

Ann Beha Architects · Anshen+Allen · Biesek Design · Cannon Design · CO Architects · Derck & Edson Associates · DiMella Shaffer · Earl Swensson Associates, Inc. (ESa) · Elkus Manfredi Architects · ELS Architecture and Urban Design · Gould Evans · GUND Partnership · Hammond Beeby Rupert Ainge Inc. · Hastings & Chivetta · HMC Architects · HOLT Architects, P.C. · Kallmann McKinnell & Wood Architects, Inc. · Perkins Eastman · Perkins+Will · Poulin + Morris Inc. · Roll • Barresi Associates · SBLD Studio · Schuler Shook · Selbert Perkins Design · Steven Holl Architects · Tai Soo Kim Partners · VOA Associates Incorporated · Yost Grube Hall Architecture · Ann Beha Architects · Anshen+Allen · Biesek Design · Cannon Design · CO Architects · Derck & Edson Associates · DiMella Shaffer · Earl Swensson Associates, Inc. (ESa) · Elkus Manfredi Architects · ELS Architecture and Urban Design · Gould Evans · GUND Partnership · Hammond Beeby Rupert Ainge Inc. · Hastings & Chivetta · HMC Architects · HOLT Architects, P.C. · Kallmann McKinnell & Wood Architects, Inc. · Perkins Eastman · Perkins+Will · Poulin + Morris Inc. · Roll • Barresi Associates · SBLD Studio · Schuler Shook · Selbert Perkins Design · Steven Holl Architects · Tai Soo Kim Partners · VOA Associates Incorporated · Yost Grube Hall Architecture · Ann Beha Architects · Anshen+Allen · Biesek Design · Cannon Design · CO Architects · Derck & Edson Associates · DiMella Shaffer · Earl Swensson Associates, Inc. (ESa) · Elkus Manfredi Architects · ELS Architecture and Urban Design · Gould Evans · GUND Partnership · Hammond Beeby Rupert Ainge Inc. · Hastings & Chivetta · HMC Architects · HOLT Architects, P.C. · Kallmann McKinnell & Wood Architects, Inc. · Perkins Eastman · Perkins+Will · Poulin + Morris Inc. · Roll • Barresi Associates · SBLD Studio · Schuler Shook · Selbert Perkins Design · Steven Holl Architects · Tai Soo Kim Partners · VOA Associates Incorporated · Yost Grube Hall Architecture · Ann Beha Architects · Anshen+Allen · Biesek Design · Cannon Design · CO Architects · Derck & Edson Associates · DiMella Shaffer · Earl Swensson Associates, Inc. (ESa) · Elkus Manfredi Architects · ELS Architecture and Urban Design · Gould Evans · GUND Partnership · Hammond Beeby Rupert Ainge Inc. · Hastings & Chivetta · HMC Architects · HOLT Architects, P.C. · Kallmann McKinnell & Wood Architects, Inc. · Perkins Eastman · Perkins+Will · Poulin + Morris Inc. · Roll • Barresi Associates · SBLD Studio · Schuler Shook · Selbert Perkins Design · Steven Holl Architects · Tai Soo Kim Partners · VOA Associates Incorporated · Yost Grube Hall Architecture · Ann Beha Architects · Anshen+Allen · Biesek Design · Cannon Design · CO Architects · Derck & Edson Associates · DiMella Shaffer · Earl Swensson Associates, Inc. (ESa) · Elkus Manfredi Architects · ELS Architecture and Urban Design · Gould Evans · GUND Partnership · Hammond Beeby Rupert Ainge Inc. · Hastings & Chivetta · HMC Architects · HOLT Architects, P.C. · Kallmann McKinnell & Wood Architects, Inc. · Perkins Eastman · Perkins+Will · Poulin + Morris Inc. · Roll • Barresi Associates · SBLD Studio · Schuler Shook · Selbert Perkins Design · Steven Holl Architects · Tai Soo Kim Partners · VOA Associates Incorporated · Yost Grube Hall Architecture · Ann Beha Architects · Anshen+Allen · Biesek Design · Cannon Design · CO Architects · Derck & Edson Associates · DiMella Shaffer · Earl Swensson Associates, Inc. (ESa) · Elkus Manfredi Architects · ELS Architecture and Urban Design · Gould Evans · GUND Partnership · Hammond Beeby Rupert Ainge Inc. · Hastings & Chivetta · HMC Architects · HOLT Architects, P.C. · Kallmann McKinnell & Wood Architects, Inc. · Perkins Eastman · Perkins+Will · Poulin + Morris Inc. · Roll • Barresi Associates · SBLD Studio · Schuler Shook · Selbert Perkins Design · Steven Holl Architects · Tai Soo Kim Partners · VOA Associates Incorporated · Yost Grube Hall Architecture · Ann Beha Architects · Anshen+Allen · Biesek Design · Cannon Design · CO Architects · Derck & Edson Associates · DiMella Shaffer · Earl Swensson Associates, Inc. (ESa) · Elkus Manfredi Architects · ELS Architecture and Urban Design · Gould Evans · GUND Partnership · Hammond Beeby Rupert Ainge Inc. · Hastings & Chivetta · HMC Architects · HOLT Architects, P.C. · Kallmann McKinnell & Wood Architects, Inc. · Perkins Eastman · Perkins+Will · Poulin + Morris Inc. · Roll • Barresi Associates · SBLD Studio · Schuler Shook · Selbert Perkins Design · Steven Holl Architects · Tai Soo Kim Partners · VOA Associates Incorporated · Yost Grube Hall Architecture · Ann Beha Architects · Anshen+Allen · Biesek Design · Cannon Design · CO Architects · Derck & Edson Associates · DiMella Shaffer · Earl Swensson Associates, Inc. (ESa) · Elkus Manfredi Architects · ELS Architecture and Urban Design · Gould Evans · GUND Partnership · Hammond Beeby Rupert Ainge Inc. · Hastings & Chivetta · HMC Architects · HOLT Architects, P.C. · Kallmann McKinnell & Wood Architects, Inc. · Perkins Eastman · Perkins+Will · Poulin + Morris Inc. · Roll • Barresi Associates · SBLD Studio · Schuler Shook · Selbert Perkins Design · Steven Holl Architects · Tai Soo Kim Partners · VOA Associates Incorporated · Yost Grube Hall Architecture · Ann Beha Architects · Anshen+Allen · Biesek Design · Cannon Design · CO Architects · Derck & Edson Associates · DiMella Shaffer · Earl Swensson Associates, Inc. (ESa) · Elkus Manfredi Architects · ELS Architecture and Urban Design · Gould Evans · GUND Partnership · Hammond Beeby Rupert Ainge Inc. · Hastings & Chivetta · HMC Architects · HOLT Architects, P.C. · Kallmann McKinnell & Wood Architects, Inc. · Perkins Eastman · Perkins+Will · Poulin + Morris Inc. · Roll • Barresi Associates · SBLD Studio · Schuler Shook · Selbert Perkins Design · Steven Holl Architects · Tai Soo Kim Partners · VOA Associates Incorporated · Yost Grube Hall Architecture · Ann Beha Architects · Anshen+Allen · Biesek Design · Cannon Design · CO Architects · Derck & Edson Associates · DiMella Shaffer · Earl Swensson Associates, Inc. (ESa) · Elkus Manfredi Architects · ELS Architecture and Urban Design · Gould Evans · GUND Partnership · Hammond Beeby Rupert Ainge Inc. · Hastings & Chivetta · HMC Architects · HOLT Architects, P.C. · Kallmann McKinnell & Wood Architects, Inc. · Perkins Eastman · Perkins+Will · Poulin + Morris Inc. · Roll • Barresi Associates · SBLD Studio · Schuler Shook · Selbert Perkins Design · Steven Holl Architects · Tai Soo Kim Partners · VOA Associates Incorporated · Yost Grube Hall Architecture · Ann Beha Architects · Anshen+Allen · Biesek Design · Cannon Design · CO Architects · Derck & Edson Associates · DiMella Shaffer · Earl Swensson Associates, Inc. (ESa) · Elkus Manfredi Architects · ELS Architecture and Urban Design · Gould Evans · GUND Partnership · Hammond Beeby Rupert Ainge Inc. · Hastings & Chivetta · HMC Architects · HOLT Architects, P.C. · Kallmann McKinnell & Wood Architects, Inc. · Perkins Eastman · Perkins+Will · Poulin + Morris Inc. · Roll • Barresi Associates · SBLD Studio · Schuler Shook · Selbert Perkins Design · Steven Holl Architects · Tai Soo Kim Partners · VOA Associates Incorporated · Yost Grube Hall Architecture

Ann Beha Architects · Anshen+Allen · Biesek Design · Cannon Design · CO Architects · Derck & Edson Associates · DiMella Shaffer · Earl Swensson Associates, Inc. (ESa) · Elkus Manfredi Architects · ELS Architecture and Urban Design · Gould Evans · GUND Partnership · Hammond Beeby Rupert Ainge Inc. · Hastings & Chivetta · HMC Architects · HOLT Architects, P.C. · Kallmann McKinnell & Wood Architects, Inc. · Perkins Eastman · Perkins+Will · Poulin + Morris Inc. · Roll • Barresi Associates · SBLD Studio · Schuler Shook · Selbert Perkins Design · Steven Holl Architects · Tai Soo Kim Partners · VOA Associates Incorporated · Yost Grube Hall Architecture · Ann Beha Architects · Anshen+Allen · Biesek Design · Cannon Design · CO Architects · Derck & Edson Associates · DiMella Shaffer · Earl Swensson Associates, Inc. (ESa) · Elkus Manfredi Architects · ELS Architecture and Urban Design · Gould Evans · GUND Partnership · Hammond Beeby Rupert Ainge Inc. · Hastings & Chivetta · HMC Architects · HOLT Architects, P.C. · Kallmann McKinnell & Wood Architects, Inc. · Perkins Eastman · Perkins+Will · Poulin + Morris Inc. · Roll • Barresi Associates · SBLD Studio · Schuler Shook · Selbert Perkins Design · Steven Holl Architects · Tai Soo Kim Partners · VOA Associates Incorporated · Yost Grube Hall Architecture · Ann Beha Architects · Anshen+Allen · Biesek Design · Cannon Design · CO Architects · Derck & Edson Associates · DiMella Shaffer · Earl Swensson Associates, Inc. (ESa) · Elkus Manfredi Architects · ELS Architecture and Urban Design · Gould Evans · GUND Partnership · Hammond Beeby Rupert Ainge Inc. · Hastings & Chivetta · HMC Architects · HOLT Architects, P.C. · Kallmann McKinnell & Wood Architects, Inc. · Perkins Eastman · Perkins+Will · Poulin + Morris Inc. · Roll • Barresi Associates · SBLD Studio · Schuler Shook · Selbert Perkins Design · Steven Holl Architects · Tai Soo Kim Partners · VOA Associates Incorporated · Yost Grube Hall Architecture · Ann Beha Architects · Anshen+Allen · Biesek Design · Cannon Design · CO Architects · Derck & Edson Associates · DiMella Shaffer · Earl Swensson Associates, Inc. (ESa) · Elkus Manfredi Architects · ELS Architecture and Urban Design · Gould Evans · GUND Partnership · Hammond Beeby Rupert Ainge Inc. · Hastings & Chivetta · HMC Architects · HOLT Architects, P.C. · Kallmann McKinnell & Wood Architects, Inc. · Perkins Eastman · Perkins+Will · Poulin + Morris Inc. · Roll • Barresi Associates · SBLD Studio · Schuler Shook · Selbert Perkins Design · Steven Holl Architects · Tai Soo Kim Partners · VOA Associates Incorporated · Yost Grube Hall Architecture · Ann Beha Architects · Anshen+Allen · Biesek Design · Cannon Design · CO Architects · Derck & Edson Associates · DiMella Shaffer · Earl Swensson Associates, Inc. (ESa) · Elkus Manfredi Architects · ELS Architecture and Urban Design · Gould Evans · GUND Partnership · Hammond Beeby Rupert Ainge Inc. · Hastings & Chivetta · HMC Architects · HOLT Architects, P.C. · Kallmann McKinnell & Wood Architects, Inc. · Perkins Eastman · Perkins+Will · Poulin + Morris Inc. · Roll • Barresi Associates · SBLD Studio · Schuler Shook · Selbert Perkins Design · Steven Holl Architects · Tai Soo Kim Partners · VOA Associates Incorporated · Yost Grube Hall Architecture · Ann Beha Architects · Anshen+Allen · Biesek Design · Cannon Design · CO Architects · Derck & Edson Associates · DiMella Shaffer · Earl Swensson Associates, Inc. (ESa) · Elkus Manfredi Architects · ELS Architecture and Urban Design · Gould Evans · GUND Partnership · Hammond Beeby Rupert Ainge Inc. · Hastings & Chivetta · HMC Architects · HOLT Architects, P.C. · Kallmann McKinnell & Wood Architects, Inc. · Perkins Eastman · Perkins+Will · Poulin + Morris Inc. · Roll • Barresi Associates · SBLD Studio · Schuler Shook · Selbert Perkins Design · Steven Holl Architects · Tai Soo Kim Partners · VOA Associates Incorporated · Yost Grube Hall Architecture · Ann Beha Architects · Anshen+Allen · Biesek Design · Cannon Design · CO Architects · Derck & Edson Associates · DiMella Shaffer · Earl Swensson Associates, Inc. (ESa) · Elkus Manfredi Architects · ELS Architecture and Urban Design · Gould Evans · GUND Partnership · Hammond Beeby Rupert Ainge Inc. · Hastings & Chivetta · HMC Architects · HOLT Architects, P.C. · Kallmann McKinnell & Wood Architects, Inc. · Perkins Eastman · Perkins+Will · Poulin + Morris Inc. · Roll • Barresi Associates · SBLD Studio · Schuler Shook · Selbert Perkins Design · Steven Holl Architects · Tai Soo Kim Partners · VOA Associates Incorporated · Yost Grube Hall Architecture · Ann Beha Architects · Anshen+Allen · Biesek Design · Cannon Design · CO Architects · Derck & Edson Associates · DiMella Shaffer · Earl Swensson Associates, Inc. (ESa) · Elkus Manfredi Architects · ELS Architecture and Urban Design · Gould Evans · GUND Partnership · Hammond Beeby Rupert Ainge Inc. · Hastings & Chivetta · HMC Architects · HOLT Architects, P.C. · Kallmann McKinnell & Wood Architects, Inc. · Perkins Eastman · Perkins+Will · Poulin + Morris Inc. · Roll • Barresi Associates · SBLD Studio · Schuler Shook · Selbert Perkins Design · Steven Holl Architects · Tai Soo Kim Partners · VOA Associates Incorporated · Yost Grube Hall Architecture · Ann Beha Architects · Anshen+Allen · Biesek Design · Cannon Design · CO Architects · Derck & Edson Associates · DiMella Shaffer · Earl Swensson Associates, Inc. (ESa) · Elkus Manfredi Architects · ELS Architecture and Urban Design · Gould Evans · GUND Partnership · Hammond Beeby Rupert Ainge Inc. · Hastings & Chivetta · HMC Architects · HOLT Architects, P.C. · Kallmann McKinnell & Wood Architects, Inc. · Perkins Eastman · Perkins+Will · Poulin + Morris Inc. · Roll • Barresi Associates · SBLD Studio · Schuler Shook · Selbert Perkins Design · Steven Holl Architects · Tai Soo Kim Partners · VOA Associates Incorporated · Yost Grube Hall Architecture · Ann Beha Architects · Anshen+Allen · Biesek Design · Cannon Design · CO Architects · Derck & Edson Associates · DiMella Shaffer · Earl Swensson Associates, Inc. (ESa) · Elkus Manfredi Architects · ELS Architecture and Urban Design · Gould Evans · GUND Partnership · Hammond Beeby Rupert Ainge Inc. · Hastings & Chivetta · HMC Architects · HOLT Architects, P.C. · Kallmann McKinnell & Wood Architects, Inc. · Perkins Eastman · Perkins+Will · Poulin + Morris Inc. · Roll • Barresi Associates · SBLD Studio · Schuler Shook · Selbert Perkins Design · Steven Holl Architects · Tai Soo Kim Partners · VOA Associates Incorporated · Yost Grube Hall Architecture · Ann Beha Architects · Anshen+Allen · Biesek Design · Cannon Design · CO Architects · Derck & Edson Associates · DiMella Shaffer · Earl Swensson Associates, Inc. (ESa) · Elkus Manfredi Architects · ELS Architecture and Urban Design · Gould Evans · GUND Partnership · Hammond Beeby Rupert Ainge Inc. · Hastings & Chivetta · HMC Architects · HOLT Architects, P.C. · Kallmann McKinnell & Wood Architects, Inc. · Perkins Eastman · Perkins+Will · Poulin + Morris Inc. · Roll • Barresi Associates · SBLD Studio · Schuler Shook · Selbert Perkins Design · Steven Holl Architects · Tai Soo Kim Partners · VOA Associates Incorporated · Yost Grube Hall Architecture · Ann Beha Architects · Anshen+Allen · Biesek Design · Cannon Design · CO Architects · Derck & Edson Associates · DiMella Shaffer · Earl Swensson Associates, Inc. (ESa) · Elkus Manfredi Architects · ELS Architecture and Urban Design · Gould Evans · GUND Partnership · Hammond Beeby Rupert Ainge Inc. · Hastings & Chivetta · HMC Architects · HOLT Architects, P.C. · Kallmann McKinnell & Wood Architects, Inc. · Perkins Eastman · Perkins+Will · Poulin + Morris Inc. · Roll • Barresi Associates · SBLD Studio · Schuler Shook · Selbert Perkins Design · Steven Holl Architects · Tai Soo Kim Partners · VOA Associates Incorporated · Yost Grube Hall Architecture